Rebuilding a Layout from A-Z

Building a better layout the second time around

Pelle K. Søeborg

KALMBACH BOOKS

Kalmbach Books
21027 Crossroads Circle
Waukesha, Wisconsin 53186
www.Kalmbach.com/Books

Published in 2012
16 15 14 13 12   1 2 3 4 5

Manufactured in the United States of America

ISBN: 978-0-89024-817-1

Photos: Photos of author on pages 56 and 103 by Ken Perry. All other photos by Pelle K. Søeborg.

Layout and design: Pelle K. Søeborg (www.soeeborg.dk)

Publisher's Cataloging-In-Publication Data

Søeborg, Pelle K.
    Rebuilding a layout from A-Z : building a better layout the second time around / Pelle K. Søeborg.

    p. : ill. (chiefly col.) ; cm. -- (Model railroader books) -- (Model railroader's how-to guide)

    Includes index.
    ISBN: 978-0-89024-817-1

    1. Railroads--Models. 2. Railroads--Models--Design and construction. I. Title. II. Title: Rebuilding a layout from A to Z
III. Series: Model railroader books.

TF197 .S642 2012
625.1/9

Contents

THE LAYOUT

The plastic pellet transfer silos were among the structures I kept from my old layout.

A switcher works undisturbed on the yard tracks in Daneville while a long heavy freight train rumbles by on the main line.

My new HO scale model railroad, Union Pacific's Daneville Subdivision, is my third layout and, in reality, an evolution of my previous Daneville & Donner River layout. Soon after that layout was finished, I began noticing things that I wished I had done differently, and during the four years that the Daneville & Donner River existed, I accumulated an extensive list of projects that I would have done in a different way if I had known better when I first built the layout.

Then one day, I came to the decision to do something about it. Some of the changes I wanted to make were so radical that it would not be possible to redo them on the existing layout, so my decision necessitated that I tear down my Daneville & Donner River layout and build a new model railroad from scratch.

There was never really any doubt in my mind that I should stay with the desert town concept as my heart belongs to Southern California and the Mojave Desert. Staying with the desert town concept allowed me to reuse many of the buildings from my old layout, which saved me a lot of time—one of the advantages of rebuilding a similar type of layout. For example, the main street with its restaurants and hotels created an excellent background. The three small rail-served businesses in Daneville also provided operational possibilities.

There are other advantages in building the same layout again. You learn from the experience of building it the first time, so you can avoid the mistakes you made. If I was building a layout featuring a totally different type of location, I would probably make new mistakes. So I assumed that building the same layout a second time would raise the odds of building a more perfect layout.

I have always modeled the present time and that was not going to change on the new layout. Since I only have room for a modest size layout, modeling the modern era with multiple locomotive lash-ups and long trains might not seem the most obvious choice. But to me, ever since 1992, when I saw an American train for the first time, U.S. railroads are long freight trains hauled by several locomotives.

Modeling the present also keeps you busy after the layout is completed because you have to update things like billboards, locomotives, and railcars. On my trips to the United States, I usually take pictures of billboards, which I then print out on my laser printer and apply to the billboard stands in Daneville. Recently, I have started upgrading all my Union Pacific locomotives with yellow sill stripes instead of red ones. In my freight car fleet, I have begun applying the yellow reflective stripes that have become common on freight cars.

Discipline is the key

Building a third layout is so much easier than building the first. When I constructed my first layout, I hardly knew where to

Highway 58 crosses over the tracks at the west end of Daneville. The overpass creates a nice entrance to the Daneville scene.

Most of the buildings in Daneville were saved from my old layout. I upgraded their old turf lawns with new fibergrass lawns before installing them on the new layout.

When you pass the Daneville railroad yard, going east on Highway 41, you get a clear view to the mainline tracks.

From time to time, I renew the billboards in Daneville to keep them current.

start or where to end. This time, I knew exactly what would be the best order of completing the tasks involved in building a model railroad. I made this layout very methodically. I first completely finished the benchwork including the subroadbed, fascia, and valance. Then, I applied sound-deadening roadbed to the entire layout, followed it with cork roadbed, laid all the track, and so on through all the steps. It can sometimes be hard to keep disciplined in completing each step before moving to the next. When I pulled and soldered all the wiring for the track and turnouts, there was a time or two when I was very tempted to leave it for a while and start on something more interesting, but I pulled myself together and finished the job, and afterwards, I was happy I did.

It is a good idea to finish each step completely before moving to the next, especially the messy ones, so you have to clean up as few times as possible. For example, I created all the plaster roads at the earliest possible stage of layout construction because sanding them smooth creates a lot of dust. That way I kept the dust problem to a minimum.

It is also much quicker to build a layout when you finish each step of the construction before moving to the next.

Nothing is perfect

I learned a lot from building this layout, especially while creating my first photographic backdrop, and I hate to say it, but I have already spotted several things on the backdrop I wish I had done differently. I am

The west end of Daneville is not the best part of town, but if you need liquor, ice, or ammo, this is where you get it.

It doesn't take much to give the feeling of a residential area. This residential area in Daneville consists of only three homes, but it still conveys the illusion of a place where families live.

sure that my next photographic backdrop will be better, and I know it is just a matter of time until I see other things I could have done differently, but that is not necessarily bad. If you are not critical of your own work, you will never improve. I think you will agree that the best feeling you can have is when you look at something you have built and say, "Wow, this really looks good." When you then try to raise the bar on your next project, you know you have succeeded if your previous project does not look so perfect anymore.

Union Pacific's Daneville Sub is, as I mentioned earlier, my third layout, and it might not be perfect, but I have managed to make a better model railroad than my previous one, and that is what counts. Someday, if I start building another layout, I know it will be better than this one. Not only because I learn from each layout I build but also because better scenery materials, structures, and trains become available all the time.

Reasons for building a new layout

One of the most important reasons for building a new layout was the high level of track noise on my old layout. I didn't pay much attention to it until I started running locomotives with sound decoders. The wheel noise from the freight cars rolling over the track almost overpowered the sound in the locomotives. Instead of laying cork roadbed directly on the subroadbed, I added a sound-deadening layer between the subroadbed and the roadbed. The material comes as 4mm-thick, asphalt-like sheets that are manufactured to lower the noise in vans. The sheets are very heavy and counteract vibrations in a car body.

I had another noise problem with a grade crossing on my old layout. Right at the center of Daneville, any train stopped

Some things will never change in Daneville. Motorists still have to pay close attention to speed restrictions, or they will get nailed by the ever-present highway patrol.

The side street containing the homes turns into a dirt road that continues into the desert.

at the siding waiting for another train blocked the crossing. The grade crossing had sound, and soon the endless ding-ding-ding got on my nerves. I decided that I would never again make a grade crossing in such an impossible place no matter how cool it looked. But what is a layout without a grade crossing? My new layout, of course, has one, but this time, I have placed it in the middle of the desert, where it can't do any harm.

There was also a time or two when I let things pass during the construction of my old layout, and it later turned out that I shouldn't have. For example, there was a particular spot on the main line where the track made a small dip. I didn't notice it until everything was ballasted and scenicked, so I let it pass instead of redoing the section. After all, I thought, it was just a cosmetic issue. Trains passed over the dip without any problems until the day I changed all my Kadee No. 5s to scale-size couplers. From that day on, I had problems with trains uncoupling at that particular spot.

One thing I was never pleased with on my old layout was the framing. In addition to not being the world's best carpenter, I made the fascia and valance from

Masonite, and it appeared too floppy for my taste. On the new Daneville layout, my ambition was to make the fascia and valance look more attractive—more museum like. My choice was MDF (medium density fiberboard). It is easy to cut, you can get it in various sizes, and you can even get special flexible MDF boards for rounded corners.

A final reason to build a new layout is simply the joy of doing it. I am a builder more than an operator, and the process of building a model railroad is what I enjoy most, especially laying track and creating scenery. Creating the benchwork is not my cup of tea, mainly because of my limitations as a carpenter, but it gives me a good feeling when the work is done, and

The guy living in the mobile home outside Daneville presumably does not like having neighbors.

Highway 41 runs along the railroad yard in Daneville. Parked on a spur there, you can find several old, out-of-service boxcars with names from long-gone railroads.

it doesn't look as bad as I feared it would. Installing and soldering all the wiring is something that just needs to be done, so there is not much joy there either, but the reward, the construction of the scenery, is waiting ahead. I really like creating scenery. Seeing a scene grow, starting with shaping the basic terrain and then by the application of rock castings, ground cover and, finally, vegetation, is a big thrill. In a few hours of work, an area can be transformed from bare plywood to a realistic-looking landscape.

Track plan

I wanted to stay with 33" radius curves and at least the same width aisles as on my old layout. I have learned that aisles need to be wide enough to accommodate multiple visitors or several operators. Taking that in consideration, the track arrangement on the new layout generally had to follow the track plan concept I developed for my previous layout with a loop and hidden staging below Daneville. I implemented a few changes though.

The new track plan included a couple of yard tracks in Daneville. The few times an operating session took place on my old Daneville layout, it became obvious that a couple of yard tracks would be nice to have when collecting and distributing freight cars from the local businesses

The little warehouse is another of the structures I saved from my old layout. The warehouse occasionally receives a boxcar with merchandise.

Nothing much is happening at the Union Pacific yard office in Daneville today. A trio of SD70ACes sit idling, but they don't seem to be going anywhere anytime soon.

and Duolith Cement. I also extended the passing siding to make it possible to run longer trains. I kept the hidden staging below Daneville as it was. Actually, that is not quite true. I had to move the turnouts in one end of the staging a few inches to fit the new track plan, but besides that, I didn't make any changes to the staging.

I used flextrack and commercial turnouts on my two previous layouts and didn't see any reason for changing that on my new layout. In my opinion, flextrack looks just as good as handlaid track when it is painted and weathered. However, I did use a different technique for painting the track on this layout.

I used three different rail sizes on my layout. For all mainline track, I used code 83. For secondary track and yards, I used code 70, and for spurs, I used code 55. To be able to run long cars troublefree, I don't use turnouts smaller than No. 6. Most of the mainline track has concrete ties.

I made a few other changes from my old layout. In the new Daneville, the

highway bridge is now located at the opposite end of town to give the highway bridge a more prominent role. A bridge over a track can be a very appealing scenic element, so moving it forward created a real eye-catching entrance to the Daneville scene. It also covered the

sharp curve the track makes just before it enters Daneville.

New industries

I reused the warehouse and the plastic pellet transfer silos from my previous layout, but I also added a new rail-served

I don't clutter my scenes with details, so I only apply just enough to create a believable scene. Behind the UP yard office, you will find a propane tank and a trashed wood pallet.

If you continue east on Highway 41, you will see the liquid asphalt transfer terminal to your left.

The liquid asphalt transfer terminal in Daneville is scratchbuilt following an old Model Railroader *article. I built the facility in order to have a place for tank cars, one of my favorite types of rolling stock.*

Historic Highway 41 out of Daneville follows the railroad most of the way and is a popular route among railfans.

business: a liquid asphalt transfer terminal. The warehouse receives boxcars, and the plastic pellet transfer facility receives hoppers, so I wanted to add some variety to the freight car consist delivered to Daneville. Because tank cars are among my favorite pieces of rolling stock, I felt that adding a place served by tank cars would be a good choice.

I couldn't find any commercially produced kits that matched what I had in mind, so I browsed through old articles to see if I could find some inspiration. I was lucky. In the February 1994 issue of *Model Railroader* magazine, Clyde B. Maybee wrote about building a liquid asphalt transfer terminal. The facility was perfect for my needs: it had an interesting and complex look, the product it made was hauled by tank cars, and it could fit the available space on my layout. Except for a few small changes, I essentially scratchbuilt my liquid asphalt transfer terminal by following this article.

As on my previous layout, Duolith Cement is my railroad's biggest customer, but the plant itself is under construction and is completely new. I have dedicated almost one-third of the layout to the cement plant to allow space for

building a better and bigger plant based on Monolith in Tehachapi, Calif. The cement plant is separated from the Daneville section of the layout by the backdrop, and it has its own access aisle, so the person operating the plant won't interfere with the person doing the switching in Daneville.

My plan is to make the structure from a combination of scratchbuilding and kitbash-

ing. I have taken lots of pictures of Monolith as reference. Of course, it will not be possible to build an exact replica of the plant, but at least it will be more realistic in size than the plant on my old layout.

The backdrop

For my new layout, I needed two backdrops: one for Daneville and one behind

Outside Daneville, Highway 41 crosses the railroad. If you want to follow the railroad from there, you have to take dirt roads.

With their refrigerating units working hard to keep up with the heat, a string of reefers travels through the desert. On a narrow scene like this, a backdrop is the only way to give a feeling of vast space.

BNSF has not assigned its newest motive power to lead this westbound manifest freight.

Tips for taking pictures of your model railroad

• Place your camera at the lowest possible trackside position.

• Use the layout's lights as a light source for even lighting on the photo.

• Use the smallest possible aperture (highest F-stop number) to get maximum depth of field. (If you want greater depth of field than the camera can provide, use photo-editing software to merge a stack of images taken with different focal points.)

the cement plant. The Daneville backdrop measures 45' × 2.5', and the cement plant backdrop measures 22' × 2.5'. The big decision used to be should I use acrylics or oil paint for my backdrop, but thanks to the digital revolution, another option emerged: the photographic backdrop. I had all the tools needed to create artwork for a photographic backdrop: a digital camera, a computer, and a photo enhancement program.

I needed pictures to work from, so I went to Southern California, the locale for my fictitious railroad, to shoot distant mountain ranges and desert scenery. I took plenty of pictures so I had enough options. I soon learned that it was not as straightforward to create the artwork as I thought. A photo backdrop may look fine on your computer screen, but when it is printed out, the colors can appear different. Before I had the entire backdrop printed out, I printed out a small section to test on my layout to see if the colors were okay. It turned out to be a good idea. I went through several test prints before I was satisfied with the colors.

The scenery

Even though my old layout was considered a desert layout, it actually had only a few feet of true desert scenery, so a bigger desert scene took priority on my new layout. I dedicated 15 feet of my layout to a single track running through pure desert scenery.

Many new scenery products have been introduced since I made my first version

A few details like this no trespassing sign make a scene much more believable.

Just before the train leaves the visible part of the layout and enters the hidden staging, it passes The Narrows, a hilly area at the end of the desert.

Service roads are as necessary for model railroads as they are for real railroads.

of Daneville, making it possible to create better-looking desert scenery. The challenge was how to make a 20"-deep scene look like a vast desert. A backdrop, of course, helped a lot, but that required making the scene blend together with the background, so the transition between the two was not noticeable. That makes modeling a desert more challenging than a scene having trees or mountains, where you can more easily hide the transition between the modeled scene and the backdrop.

For creating the basic terrain, I used foam insulation board, which in my opinion is superior to any other product. It is strong and easy to work with. I also used foam insulation board for the terrain on my previous layout and on several dioramas, and for me, it works much better than the old plaster cloth on chicken wire method.

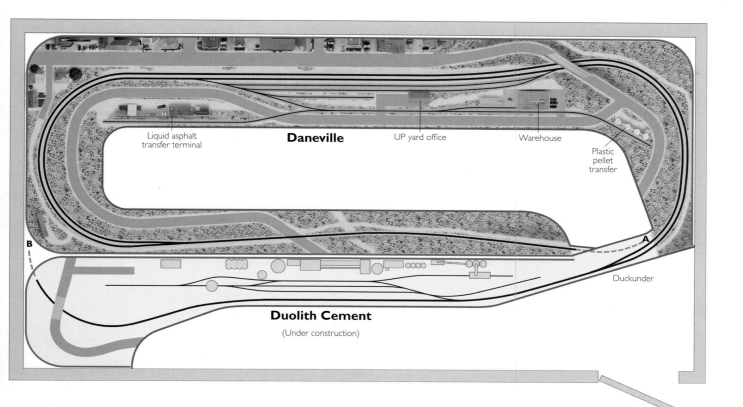

Liquid asphalt transfer terminal

Daneville

UP yard office

Warehouse

Plastic pellet transfer

B

A

Duckunder

Duolith Cement

(Under construction)

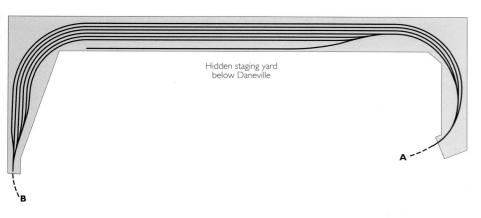

Hidden staging yard below Daneville

A

B

Streets and highways

After track, roads play the most prominent role on my layout. Roads are a wonderful scenic element. You can use them to cut through the scenery and create viewing lines on your layout and also use them to divide scenes.

My layout is covered with roads. The widest road is the main street in Daneville—an almost 14-foot-long, three-lane street. Then, there are the highways. One of them goes over the top of the track and creates a great scene divider. Another parallels the track for more than 22 feet before it crosses the track and disappears in the distance. The smallest roads on my layout are the service roads that run along almost every inch of mainline railroad track.

I have a passion for roads as roads have taken me to all my railroad adventures: not always paved roads but also dirt roads and sometimes just trails. My layout is designed from a railfan's perspective, and I can't imagine making a model railroad without roads, so I include them when I start sketching track plans to make sure to allow space for them.

On the following pages, I will explain each step of the construction of my new Daneville layout.

Layout at a glance

Name: Union Pacific Daneville Subdivision

Scale: HO

Size: 11 x 22 feet

Prototype: UP and BNSF

Locale: Freelanced inspired by the Mojave Desert in Southern California

Era: Present

Layout Style: Walk-in

Mainline run: 59 feet (excluding staging)

Minimum radius: 33" on main line, 31" on siding

Tunouts: Main line No. 8, sidings and yards No. 6

Maximum Grade: 2.3 percent

Height: 50" to 58"

Scenery: Foam insulation board

Backdrop: Photographic

Control: Lenz DCC

BUILDING BENCHWORK

Before I started on the benchwork, I installed the lighting for the layout. The lighting consists of a series of fluorescent lamps mounted behind the valance. It is easier to mount the lamps before the benchwork is constructed because you have easier access to the lamps when you install them, and I was able to position a step ladder right below the lights. That way I also had excellent working light when I constructed the benchwork and the layout itself. I use full-spectrum fluorescent light tubes with

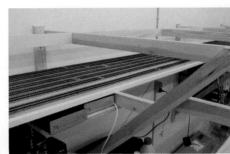

The staging below Daneville is the only thing from my old Daneville layout I kept. I had to make a new framework for Daneville as the scene is 3" deeper than on my old layout.

A view across the room with the freestanding section in the foreground and the Daneville area with the staging below in the background. I used 1 x 2s for the frame construction and 2 x 2s for the center posts in the freestanding section.

A view under the freestanding section. Having center posts instead of legs on each side of the frame makes the aisles feel wider.

a color temperature of 4000° Kelvin. This color temperature provides cool light, which produces higher contrast and is preferred for visual tasks. These lights are often used in butcher shops because they make the meat look fresh and savory.

I have to admit I am not a skilled carpenter—far from it. I do my best, but I know my work does not reach professional standards. I have learned one thing though: it pays to use high-quality materials for your benchwork. Remember, it is the only thing on your layout that is almost impossible to change later on if you are not pleased with it.

From my previous layout, I learned that you don't need to use heavy lumber to obtain sturdy benchwork. A lightweight wood

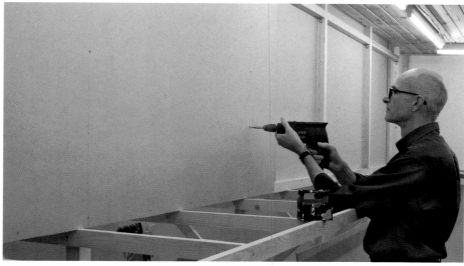

I mounted ¼" medium density fiberboard (MDF) back to back on the posts as a scene divider and as a base for the backdrop.

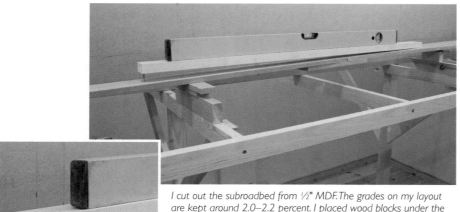

I cut out the subroadbed from ½" MDF. The grades on my layout are kept around 2.0–2.2 percent. I placed wood blocks under the subroadbed to build up the grades. I used a homemade tool to measure the exact grade. The tool consists of a 1-meter-long board with a screw attached to one end and a carpenter's level placed on top of it. How long the screw sticks out defines the steepness of the grade. If it sticks out 2cm, the grade is 2 percent on a level board.

Making level roadbed

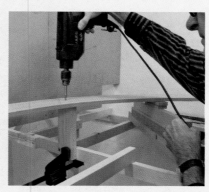

1. When the grade is established, the wood pieces I used for shimming the subroadbed are replaced with risers. I clamped the risers to the benchwork and attached them to the subroadbed with screws.

2. Next, I placed a carpenter's level across the top of the subroadbed, loosened the clamp, and twisted the riser until the subroadbed was level. Then I attached the riser to the benchwork.

A view of the 2.2 percent grade on the future desert scene. Where sections of subroadbed join, I glued an extra piece of MDF below to reinforce the joint.

The valance was made of ⅓" MDF. I painted the boards white on the back side before mounting them. White reflects the light better, which will improve the lighting on the layout. I mounted the valance to triangular pieces of ½" MDF. In addition to serving as supports for the valance, they also serve as view blocks for the fluorescent light tubes.

frame along with foam insulation board for the terrain provides stable enough bench-work. I used 1 × 2s for the frame construction and 2 × 2s for posts in the freestanding section.

I wanted to create more open space under the layout, which makes the aisles feel wider. Along the walls, I attached the bench-work to it. The freestanding section is supported by 2 × 2 floor-to-ceiling wood posts that eliminate the use of additional legs.

Fascia and valance

On my previous layout, I used Masonite for the fascia and valance, and I was never pleased with their floppy appearance, which was especially apparent when anyone leaned on the valance. On my new layout, I wanted the framing to look more

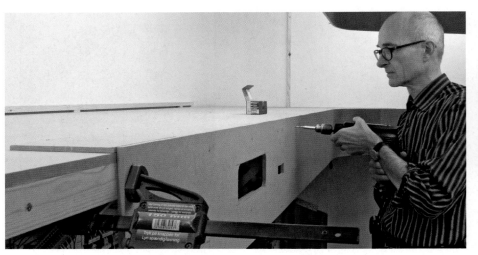

The unfortunately unavoidable duckunder on my layout will not be removable. On my old layout, I originally had a removable duckunder, but it created a lot of problems, and I ended up attaching it to the layout permanently, so this time, I made a permanently fixed duckunder from the beginning.

The fascia was also made from ⅓" MDF. I made the holes for the control panels and DCC connectors before mounting the fascia to the benchwork with screws.

When the fascia was mounted, I drew the contour of the landscape on it. If you don't have a clear vision of how you want your landscape to look, you can always do this later. I just prefer to get all the sawing over with first because of all the dust it creates.

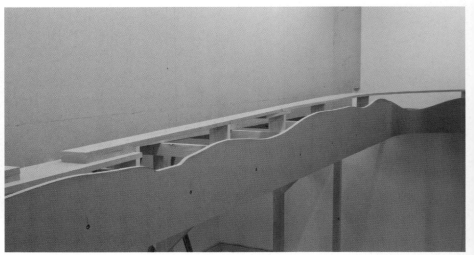

This picture shows the fascia in front of the desert scene with the landscape contour cut out. All that remained for the model railroad carpenter to finish was sanding the edges of the fascia smooth.

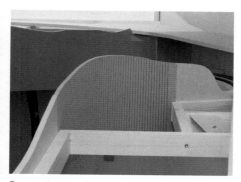

For creating rounded corners, you can buy special pieces of MDF. The boards have parallel grooves on the back side that make it possible for you to bend the board. The minimum radius on my round corners is 22", which is about as tight a radius as you can get.

museum-like, so I went to the building supply store to see what I could find. My choice was medium density fiberboard (MDF). MDF is easy to cut, you can get it in various sizes, and special flexible boards are available for rounded corners.

I first painted the fascia and valance in a white primer. Then, I sanded the primed surface smooth before applying the final color. I like the fascia and valance in a darker color than the scenery—much darker—as it

frames the scenes in a very appealing way. I have seen layouts where the fascia has been painted in almost the same color as the scenery, and in a way it expands the scene, but I prefer the contrast. It makes the modeled scene stand out in a more dramatic way. Because I model the Southern California desert, my scenery is dominated by warm burnt shades. To provide a contrast, I selected a warm gray color, which provided a dark gray frame for my desert scene.

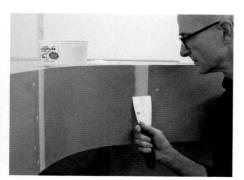

I smoothed out all the joints and screwheads on the valance and fascia with plaster.

I covered the valance and fascia with a flat white primer. After the paint dried, I sanded the surface lightly to prepare it for the final coat.

This view down the other side of the freestanding section shows where my scratchbuilt cement plant will be located.

The valance and fascia received several coats of a dark gray satin paint. I chose a warm shade of gray that would better highlight the burnt colors of my desert scenery.

LAYING TRACK

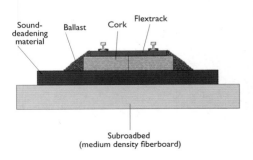

Sound-deadening material · Ballast · Cork · Flextrack

Subroadbed
(medium density fiberboard)

One of the main reasons for my decision to rebuild my Daneville layout from scratch was the high level of track noise on my old layout. I hadn't paid much attention to it until I started using locomotives with sound decoders and discovered that the wheel noise from the freight cars rolling over the track almost overpowered the sound of the locomotives. Fortunately, my good friend Flemming Ørneholm had solved the track noise problem on his layout, so I simply borrowed his idea of adding a sound-deadening layer between the subroadbed and the roadbed. The material I used comes as 4mm-thick asphalt-based panels that is meant for reducing the noise in automobiles and other vehicles. The material is very heavy and counteracts the vibrations in a car body.

I cut the panels in strips of various widths: 2"-wide strips for straight track and 1/3"-wide strips for curves. Under multiple tracks, I used pieces that matched the total width of the tracks. Flemming also applied a layer of foam rubber from an exercise mat under the material, but I skipped that step and applied the strips directly on the MDF (medium density fiberboard) subroadbed hoping it would be sufficient to reduce the noise enough to give the sound decoders a chance. I don't mind some wheel noise as long as I also can hear the locomotive sounds. After all, trains are not silent.

The self-adhesive, sound-deadening material is easy to apply. You need to clean off all sawdust from the surface before you attach the pieces, or they won't stick properly.

The material is coated with a thin cling film. I was afraid that the glue I use for ballast wouldn't stick properly to the film, so I removed it. I don't know if this was necessary, but I didn't want to take any chances.

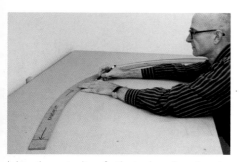

I drew the center lines for the track on the subroadbed at the Daneville area, utilizing my homemade "curve-with-easement ruler" that has a 33" radius curve on the outside and a 31" radius curve on the inside.

The film was not easy to remove. It has a tendency to come apart when you pull it, so I could only remove small pieces at a time. I found out that if you heat the surface with a hair dryer first, the film becomes easier to remove.

After my layout was finished, we test-ran two different locomotives on Flemming's layout and then on mine to see how much difference the layer of foam rubber on Flemming's layout made. On Flemming's layout, there was almost no wheel noise at all. On my layout, you could hear wheel noise but not in any annoying way. It was a deeper and more pleasant sound than on my previous layout.

The conclusion is that if you prefer totally silent track, you can follow Flemming's method and add a soft layer of foam rubber followed by a layer of sound-deadening material under the cork roadbed. If you don't mind some wheel noise, a layer of sound-deadening

I applied the sound-deadening strips to the subroadbed. The asphalt-based sheets are self-adhesive, so you just remove the backing paper and apply it. Make sure that the surface you apply it to is free from dust.

material is sufficient. If the sharp metallic sound of wheels doesn't bother you, you can attach the roadbed directly to the subroadbed without any other materials under it.

The room size also makes a difference in how you perceive the sound. The smaller the room, the more noticeable the sound will be.

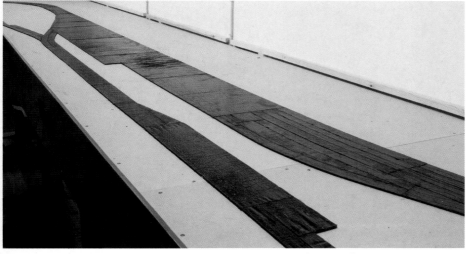

This picture shows the Daneville area with the sound-deadening material in place. On straight areas with multiple tracks, I used larger sheets instead of strips.

The sound-deadening material does not bend easily, so I made the curves from many narrow strips instead of a few wide ones.

Cutting sound-deadening material

1. I cut the sound-deadening, asphalt-based sheets into strips. The material is hard to cut, so I only cut about one-third of the way through the sheet. In order to not disturb the backing paper, I cut them from the back side.

2. I made strips of various widths, which separate easily. The material is fairly rigid, so I made a number of narrow strips for the curves since they would be easier to shape than wider strips.

3. The asphalt-based material is coated with a thin cling film. I was afraid that the glue wouldn't stick properly to the film, so I removed it. The film is easier to remove if you first heat the surface with a hair dryer.

4. Pull off the film while the strip is still warm and soft. If it cools, the film has a tendency to come off in small pieces.

Roadbed

Cork is my preferred roadbed. It is easy to cut and sand, it is flexible, and it holds spikes well. You can use several types of cork, with different properties, for roadbed. For previous layouts, I have used cork for flooring, which is a hard type of cork. This time, I used a very soft type of cork because I thought it would make the trains even quieter. It was also very easy to cut and shape.

I bought the cork in large sheets and cut it into strips. For straight track, I cut 1.4"-wide strips that covered the width of the track. For curves, I cut the strips

I used cork as roadbed for my track. I used an all-purpose glue to apply the cork to the sound-deadening material.

On curves, I pinned the cork strips in place until the glue dried.

I made simple spacers from styrene to keep the cork roadbed spaced consistently.

I used a wider spacer to align parallel curves, which are a little farther apart than my parallel straightaways. This ensures clearance for long cars when they pass each other.

Cutting roadbed for turnouts

1. Place the turnout on a sheet of cork. Draw the contour of the turnout on the cork with a pen.

2. Cut out the piece with a sharp hobby knife, making it slightly wider than the turnout.

Making smooth transitions

1. There is a height difference between the roadbed I used on the main line and on the siding. I used ¹³⁄₆₄" (5mm) cork for the main line and ⅛" (3mm) for sidings.

2. I sanded the transition area between the main line and siding smooth. You can do it by hand, but using a power sander will save you a lot of time.

3. Make sure that the transition is long and smooth. If it is too steep, there is a risk that your trains will uncouple when they run over the area.

in half the width, so they could be bent to fit the curve radius more easily. In rail yards, I laid sheets wide enough to go under all of the tracks. For turnouts, I cut custom pieces of cork to fit under each turnout.

Mainline track has higher ballast than does secondary track, so I used two different thicknesses of cork: ¹³⁄₆₄" (5mm) for the main line and ⅛" (3mm) for sidings and yards.

I glued the cork on top of the subroadbed using ordinary all-purpose glue, but

you can also use latex caulk for this purpose. To avoid bulges caused by pockets of glue under the cork, I pressed the cork roadbed down by rolling a bottle over it several times. A paste roller is an even better tool for this.

I finished placing all the roadbed on my layout before I started laying any track, as this view of the finished roadbed in Daneville shows.

The yard for the cement plant has received a layer of cork on top of the sound-deadening layer.

Laying the track

I enjoy laying track very much. I find it very relaxing. Your mind wanders while you are working, and you get all kinds of ideas. As on my two previous layouts, I used flextrack on my new layout as well. When it is painted and weathered, flex-

I didn't glue my track to the cork but attached it only with spikes. That way I can easily adjust a section of track simply by pulling up a couple of spikes.

track provides a very realistic appearance. There are many brands of flextrack available, and Micro Engineering is my preferred brand because it offers a nice selection of rail sizes. I use three different rail sizes on my layout. For all mainline track, I use code 83. For secondary track and yards, I use code 70, and for spurs, I use code 55.

I didn't glue my track to the cork, but mounted it with spikes only. That way, I can, if necessary, easily readjust a section of track simply by pulling up a couple of spikes, adjusting the track, and pushing the spikes down again.

I solder the joints on every second section of track. Temperature and humidity are constantly changing where I live, so on the rest of the joints, I leave small gaps for expansion. To ensure reliable operation, I solder feeder wires to every section of track.

Superelevated curves

The long curves on my layout are superelevated. To raise the outer ties, I glue a small piece of styrene under every ninth tie. I make gradual changes of elevation by inserting .010"-thick styrene pieces under the first 8" of track, then placing .020"-thick styrene under the next 8" of track, followed by .030" styrene, and ending with .040" styrene for the highest elevation. This creates a nice long and smooth approach to the elevation. A steeper rise in elevation can cause derailments, especially with long locomotives. I did not superelevate the short curves on my layout due to the steep rise that would be needed.

Superelevated curves do not improve how trains operate on the track. Actually, they can make it more troublesome. Long double-stack trains have an tendency to tilt too much when they are pulled through a superelevated curve (although adding weight to the lower containers can prevent this problem). The only reasonable argument for having superelevated curves on a model railroad is that it looks so cool when a train glides through the curves.

Between every second section of flextrack, I left a small gap in the rails for expansion. To ensure that the distance was exactly the same on all gaps, I used a piece of styrene strip as a spacer.

The most reliable way of checking to see if your track is straight or a curve is smooth is by looking down the track from a low angle, which will reveal even the slightest kink.

To make superelevated curves, I glued a small piece of styrene under every ninth tie. I made a gentle change of elevation by adding pieces of styrene under the track: starting with .010" pieces under the first 8" of track, .020" under the next 8" of track, then .030", and finally .040" for the highest elevation.

I made a simple tool from styrene to space the tracks consistently. The distance between the centers of the tracks is 15 scale feet in curves and 13.5 scale feet on straight track.

Adding feeder wires to track

1. To ensure reliable operation on my layout, I connected feeder wires to every section of track. I drilled the holes for the wires through the roadbed as close to the rails as possible.

2. The joints between every second section of flextrack were soldered together. I also soldered the feeder wires to these joints. That way, one set of feeder wires can power two sections of flextrack.

3. After the wires were connected to the rails, I slipped a couple of ties under the rails.

On the subject of curves, the biggest compromise on my layout is that I had to settle for a 33" radius for mainline curves and a 31" radius for the passing siding in Daneville. Neither radius is optimal for running modern equipment with freight cars up to 90 feet long. I hate sharp curves and will do almost anything to get wide curves, but the physical dimensions of my train room set the limits. I have managed to keep the sharpness of my curves less noticeable by keeping the height of the layout around 55–57 inches.

Test your track

I did some thorough test-running on my newly laid track to make sure that there were no mysterious derailments or dead spots. I set up the worst possible consist of cars for the test-run with long 90-foot autoracks coupled next to short 60-foot cars. I knew that if this train could make it without any problems, any train could do it.

On less-used track, there is often a greater distance between the ties than on mainline track. You can simulate this by cutting the connectors between the ties and then pushing the ties a little farther apart.

The upper track shown is code 55 used for a spur and the other track is code 70 as a yard track. Note that the ties on the spur are spaced farther apart than on the yard track.

When I connect rails of different heights, I squeeze the rail joiner on the tallest rail flat and solder the lower rail on top of it.

I used three different rail sizes on my layout. For all mainline track, I used code 83. For secondary track and yards, I used code 70, and for spurs, I used code 55. The track in the foreground is code 55, and the track at center is code 70.

Modifying a Peco turnout

The switch points are made from a folded piece of metal instead of a solid rail. Where the point touches the stock rail, there is a notch where the folded layer becomes a single layer. I filled this area with solder to make a smoother transition.

To minimize the gap between the stock rail and the open points, I made a new switch rod from styrene strip. I soldered a piece of flat brass bar under each of the switch points to provide a surface to glue the switch rod to. I then glued them together with cyanoacrylate adhesive.

I also trimmed the head block ties (the extended ties for the switch stand) since they were too wide. I filled the holes meant for Peco's snap-on switch machines with styrene (shown by the two white dots). I removed the section with the spring mechanism and replaced it with a piece of styrene strip (the white tie next to the throw bar).

Turnouts

I use commercially made turnouts on my layout. There are so many variations and brands to choose from that you can make almost any track layout you want. To create smoother tracks in yards and other places where the space is limited, some trimming of the turnouts may be required.

Most of the turnouts on my layout are No. 6 turnouts from Micro Engineering. These turnouts come with a couple of add-on details such as frog bolt head plates and guard rail clamps.

The other type of turnouts I use are No. 8s from Peco. I placed these turnouts in

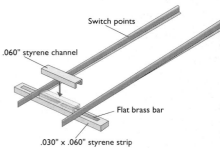

The drawing shows how the new switch rod system was made for my Peco turnouts. The styrene channel attached on top of the throw bar adds extra strength to the joint between the switch points and the throw bar.

Replacing a throw bar spring

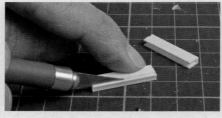

1. I made bushings from Evergreen .125" x .250" rectangular tubes. I cut the pieces into lengths that matched the total thickness of the roadbed or baseboard.

2. One tube is not wide enough to accommodate the movements of the spring wire, so I had to fashion one from two pieces. I first trimmed off one side of a tube piece.

3. Then I glued the two pieces together and ended up with a rectangular tube wide enough to handle the movements of the spring wire.

4. I drilled a series of holes through the roadbed right next to each other, so they created a rectangular hole wide enough for the bushing.

5. I slid the bushing in the hole.

6. My bushing was press-fit, but if it is too loose, you can secure it with a dab of glue.

each end of the passing siding at Daneville. I used Peco turnouts there because Micro Engineering does not make turnouts larger than No. 6. The Peco turnouts had some visual imperfections that I decided to change. A too-large gap between the stock rail and the open point is very noticeable, especially if you take pictures of your layout from a low angle. The throw bar section with the head block ties also looked a little too massive, so I trimmed a portion and replaced the rest with parts made from styrene strips.

Newer Micro Engineering turnouts are ready for DCC. The frog is insulated, so you can wire it for switched polarity. Peco turnouts with Electrofrog are factory-wired for DCC.

When you lay a series of turnouts close together, such as in a yard, you get a lot of joints. You can minimize the number of joints by splicing the turnouts. You do that by pulling out a frog rail from each of the two turnouts you want to splice together. When you trim the length of the turnouts, leave a stock rail long enough on each turnout to fit into the space of the removed frog rail on the opposite turnout and push the two turnouts together. I have only tried this method on Micro Engineering turnouts, and for other brands, it will depend on how the frog rails are shaped and attached. On Micro Engineering turnouts, the frog rails are not part of the frog. The frog rails butt up against a cast frog and are relatively easy to remove.

My turnouts are operated by Tortoise switch machines, so the little spring on Micro Engineering turnouts that presses the switch points against the stock rail is not needed, so I removed them on all my Micro Engineering turnouts. The Peco turnouts have a spring mechanism too, but on them, I replaced the entire throw bar section, including the part with the spring, with pieces made from styrene strips instead.

Splicing turnouts

1. First, pull out a frog rail from each of the turnouts. Be careful not to damage the little taps that hold the rail. The Micro Engineering frog rails can be detached from the frog. The frog rails butt up against a cast frog and are, therefore, relatively easy to remove.

2. Then trim the turnouts. Cut the rails except for the stock rail on each turnout that corresponds with the frog rail you just removed.

3. Trim off the unnecessary section of ties with a sharp knife.

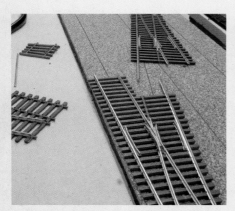

4. Finally, trim the long stock rail on each turnout to fit to the exact length of the space of the removed frog rail on the opposite turnout. Both turnouts are now trimmed and ready to be spliced.

5. Push the two turnouts together. Be very careful not to damage the little taps in the ties when you slide the rails under them. I ruined one turnout pushing them together.

6. The two turnouts are now spliced together without any joints. Not only does it look better, but it provides more reliable train operation.

Painting track

Paint makes a world of difference to the look of flextrack. I model present time, so on my layout, most of the mainline track has concrete ties. Only on a small stretch of track on the desert area opposite Daneville does the main line have wood ties. All secondary track and yard tracks have wood ties.

The concrete mainline track received a coat of concrete color applied with an airbrush. My concrete color consisted of equal amounts of Model Master Gull Gray, Sand, and white. I brush-painted the rail and the clips holding the rail in a grimy grayish-brown color mixed from three parts Dark Drab, three parts Dark Skin, and one part Gull Gray. Painting the rails is tedious and boring work, but it is worth the effort. I weathered the concrete ties along the rails using brown powdered chalk applied with a soft brush.

For tracks and turnouts with wood ties, I gave them a base coat of light gray applied with an airbrush. I made a tie color from one part Vallejo Model Air 042 Cam Black Brown and one part 055 Gray Green. I thinned the mix to a wash with water and a little rubbing alcohol and applied it to the ties. Secondary track and sidings received a single coat while mainline track received two coats.

This method is, of course, more time consuming than just airbrushing everything in the same brownish color, which looks all right too. I did that on my previ-

Painting track with concrete ties

1. With my airbrush, I gave all concrete track a couple of coats of my concrete blend, which consists of Model Master Gull Gray, Sand, and white in equal amounts.

2. Because I painted all concrete track in the same workflow, the paint had time to dry before I could remove it from the top of the rails, so I had to scrape the paint off with a sharp chisel blade.

3. I dipped a piece of cloth in thinner and rubbed it against the top of the rail to remove the last residues of paint.

4. I brush-painted the rail and rail clips in a grayish-brown color mixed from three parts Model Master Dark Drab, three parts Dark Skin, and one part Gull Gray. This step is time consuming and made me envy people modeling eras before concrete track.

5. Finally, I weathered the concrete track along the rails with brown powdered chalk. I didn't seal the chalk with varnish as the chalk adhered very well to the flat paint.

Before I started painting the track, I slipped small pieces of foam insulation board between the open switch point and stock rail on all turnouts to prevent paint from interfering with the electrical contact between the parts.

To suck up most of the paint dust, I clamped the hose from a vacuum cleaner to the benchwork and turned on the vacuum cleaner while I used the airbrush.

ous layout and was pleased with the results, but adding a wash over a gray primer gives the ties a more realistic wood look.

The rails on secondary track and sidings were brush-painted with a grimy grayish-brown color mixed from two parts Model Master Dark Drab and one part Gull Gray. The mainline rail received the same color as the concrete did.

One problem with painting flextrack is that the ties are made from a slick type of plastic that paint doesn't stick very well to and, therefore, can be scratched easily. Especially when you apply ballast, you have to be careful not to brush too hard when you spread it as you can scrape off some of the paint on the ties.

Weathering the track

Rails and ties, especially the concrete ones, need a little weathering to look realistic. I applied some brown powdered chalk along the rails with a soft brush. The wood ties don't need any additional weathering as painting them with a light gray base coat and a stain gives them a nice weathered look. On some of the turnouts, I applied rust-colored powder to the tie plates and other "metal" parts. I didn't find it necessary to seal the chalk with varnish as the chalk sticks very well to the flat paint.

On turnouts, I applied rust-colored powder to the tie plates and other "metal" parts.

Painting track with wood ties

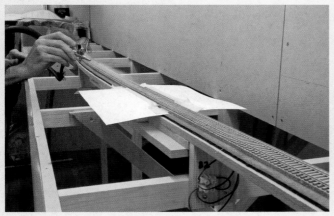

1. I airbrushed ties and rails light gray, but first I covered an already-installed trestle with paper to protect it from the spray.

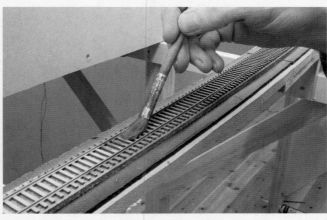

2. After the paint dried, I gave the ties a stain mixed from equal amounts of Vallejo 042 Cam Black Brown and 055 Gray Green thinned with water and a little rubbing alcohol. Newer ties received two coats, and older ties received only one coat, so they appeared more grayish.

3. I brush-painted the rail on the secondary track and sidings with a grimy grayish-brown color mixed from two parts Model Master Dark Drab and one part Gull Gray. The mainline rail received the same color as the concrete.

4. This close-up of the track shows how painting with a light gray base color and a grayish-brown stain brings out the wood details of the ties.

TERRAIN

After the track had been laid, it was time to start on the scenery. The first step was to create the subterrain. I started by planning where the roads should be placed in the scenes. I made subroads from ¼" medium density fiberboard (MDF). The purpose of the subroads is to create a nice even surface for the pavement, which consists of plaster. I made all the subroads on the layout before I started on the basic terrain.

For the level Daneville area, above the staging, I simply drew the outlines of the subroads directly on ¼" MDF and cut out road sections with a jigsaw. I placed these sections on the boards that made up the base for Daneville and fastened the subroad sections with screws.

On the rest of the layout, where there was open benchwork and the roads were supposed to follow the landscape contours, I first made a layout for the road using pieces of cardboard taped together to get an general idea of how it would look.

Subroads, made of ¼"-thick MDF (medium density fiberboard) are applied to the Daneville area. Here, you can see what is going to be Highway 41 to the left and the parking lot for the yard office to the right.

In places where the road crosses the track, I had to trim the edges of the subroad to keep the road surface level with the rails.

MDF is easy to trim. I simply used a sharp hobby knife for this purpose.

I filled the area between the main street and the track with a lightweight putty. I applied it so the layer is thinnest towards the center.

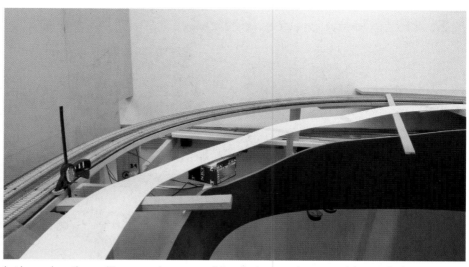

In places where the road is supposed to curve or follow the landscape's contours, I first made the road layout from pieces of cardboard taped together to get a general idea of how it would look.

When I was pleased with the road layout, I used the cardboard road as a template for cutting the subroad sections. The subroad sections were screwed and glued to the benchwork.

At the highway overpass at the west end of Daneville, the subroad had to be raised to the height of the bridge. I made risers in different sizes from MDF leftovers and glued them to the layout. When the glue was dry, I glued the subroad to the risers in two steps. I first glued the subroad to the riser closest to the bridge.

When I was pleased with the layout of the roads, I used cardboard as a template for cutting the subroad. I used ¼"-thick MDF for the subroad. The ¼" boards can be bent to follow the landscape contours. I held the subroad in place with clamps and then screwed and glued it to the benchwork.

In Daneville, the old highway runs along the edge of the layout, and there was a small gap between the subroad and the fascia that I filled with Woodland Scenics Foam Putty. I covered the top edge of the fascia with masking tape first.

On the other side of the highway, between the subroad and the track, there also was a little gap, which I filled with the foam putty.

To create a small ditch, I pulled the rounded side of a spatula through the wet putty.

Stacking foam pieces vertically

1. Place a piece of foam vertically in the area you want to fill. Outline the desired shape on the foam piece. On the side facing away, outline the contour of the terrain next to it.

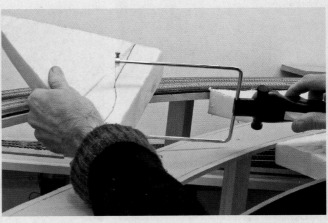

2. Cut along the pencil line. A hot wire foam cutter is by far the best tool for this cutting job.

3. Glue the foam piece to the layout. I used an all-purpose glue found at the local building supply store.

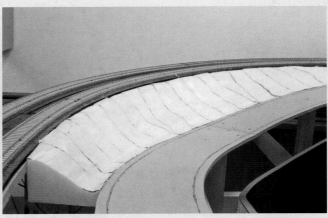

4. Add additional pieces the same way as the first until the entire area is filled with small vertical foam pieces.

5. Sand all the joints and cutting marks smooth with a piece of coarse sandpaper. This creates a lot of electrostatic granulate, so it is a good idea to have a vacuum ready for cleanup.

6. Fill any gaps with a lightweight putty. I used Woodland Scenics Foam Putty, which you can find at hobby dealers, and a similar product that I found at a local building supply store.

I waited until the glue had dried completely and then applied glue to the rest of the risers and forced the subroad down. I fastened the opposite end of the ramp to the layout with screws.

For creating the basic terrain, foam insulation board is superior to any other product. I used foam insulation board for the terrain on my previous layout and on a several dioramas, and for me, it works better than the old method of covering chicken wire with plaster cloth. Foam insulation board also has the advantage of functioning as an integrated part of the benchwork. It is very rigid and stabilizes the benchwork and makes it sturdier.

There are various ways of making terrain from foam insulation board. You can precut blocks and stack them on top of each other like a sandwich and then cut the terrain

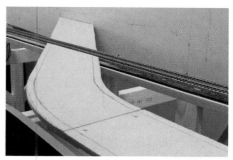

Grade crossings always attract attention, and my railroad, of course, had to have one, so I added a curve to the highway, allowing it to cross the tracks.

Adding a highway overpass ramp

1. At the highway overpass, the subroad had to be raised. I first glued a series of risers to the layout and let the glue dry. I then glued the subroad to the risers in two steps. I first glued the subroad to the riser closest to the bridge. After it was dry, I applied glue to the rest of the risers and forced the roadbed down and screwed the opposite end of the ramp to the layout. For more on the highway bridge, go to page 76.

2. It was not possible to make the odd-shaped ramp where old Highway 41 joined Highway 58 from MDF, so I made it from a piece of foam insulation board instead.

3. I shaped the slopes from pieces of foam insulation board and attached them with all-purpose glue.

4. I made the Highway 41 junction from a solid piece of foam board. I drew a line along the edge of the blue ramp.

5. With a sharp knife, I shaped the terrain and glued the piece in place.

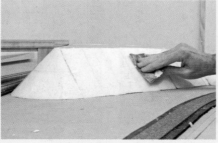

6. I placed a second piece on top of the first and repeated the procedure.

7. I sanded all the joints smooth with a piece of coarse sandpaper.

8. The final step was to fill any gaps with a lightweight putty.

Creating basic terrain for a desert scene

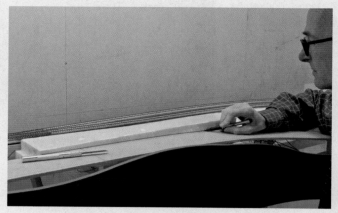

1. I trimmed the width on a block of foam to fit the gap between the track and the highway. I then drew the contour of the highway on the foam.

2. I shaped the terrain contours with a flexible saw. It is easier to do the trimming before the foam block is glued in place.

3. The shaped foam block is back in place and glued to the layout. Note the notch at the end of the terrain. The next section will have a corresponding notch and will rest on the first section.

4. I continued filling the area on both sides of the highway with foam terrain.

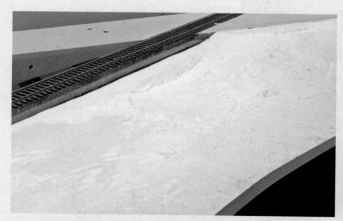

5. Although deserts may seem flat, there are height variations in the terrain. Where the terrain is lower than the track, the railroad will make a fill. Such things are easy to cut out in foam.

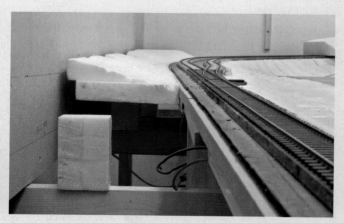

6. I used foam blocks as risers to support the foam terrain on the other side of the track. Because the backdrop was not yet installed, I left a small gap between the terrain and the wall.

The terrain around the trestle is made from several smaller pieces of foam. I started by roughly cutting out the banks with a long-bladed hobby knife. For building the trestle, see page 74.

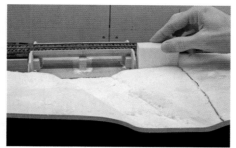

I filled the areas behind the trestle's end walls with small foam blocks and cut them to shape.

I sanded all joints and cutting marks smooth with a piece of coarse sandpaper and filled the gaps with foam putty.

Shaping a hill

1. Most of the desert scene is so shallow that the terrain could be shaped from a single layer of 2" foam insulation board, but where the scene ends, there is a little hill that required more than one layer.

2. I tested a precut foam block to see if it fit the corner.

3. I then roughly shaped the foam block into a hill and glued it in place.

contours, or you can cut the terrain profiles before you stack them. A third way is to cut the terrain profiles and place them next to each other vertically. This method works well for creating rugged terrain and is also a good way to use all the odd pieces left over from other modeling projects. I used all three methods on my layout.

Working with foam

I used various tools to cut foam insulation board including a hot-wire cutter, a saw with a flexible blade, a serrated bread knife and a foam knife from Woodland Scenics.

I glued the foam pieces together with an all-purpose glue. Test your glue on a piece of foam first to make sure that the glue

doesn't attack the foam. I used long pins called foam nails to hold the foam blocks together until the glue has dried.

I filled any gaps with foam putty. Finally, I sanded all joints and cutting marks smooth with a piece of coarse sandpaper.

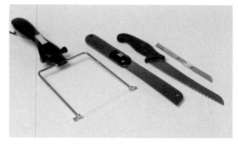

The tools I use for cutting foam insulation board are a hot wire cutter, a flexible saw, a serrated knife, and a long-bladed hobby knife.

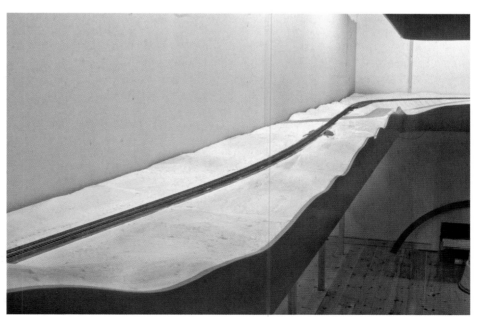

This is the desert terrain as it looked before any ground cover was applied. The foam insulation board layer is strong and makes the entire benchwork construction sturdier.

Creating basic terrain for a hilly scene with a tunnel

1. In the corner behind the cement plant where the track disappears into the staging, I premade sections of subterrain first and glued them in place.

2. I made a tunnel to hide the entrance to the staging yard.

3. I filled the area between the yard for the cement plant and the main line with precut foam blocks placed vertically next to each other.

4. The space between the main line and the highway were filled with blocks of foam stacked like a sandwich. I glued the foam with an all-purpose adhesive.

5. When the glue had dried, I shaped the terrain contours roughly with my bread knife.

6. I continued filling the area with foam blocks and shaped the terrain with various tools.

I cleaned the surface with a vacuum cleaner to remove foam pieces and sanding dust. Before adding scenery, I gave the entire subterrain a coat of earth-colored latex paint. The paint created a neutral-colored base for the ground cover.

Creating basic terrain for the desert

Although deserts may seem flat, there are variations in the terrain, so forget about making a desert from a sheet of plywood. The desert terrain I was going to make was relatively flat, so most of it could be shaped from a single layer of 2"-thick foam. The only exception was in a corner where there was a large gap between the track and the highway below. To fill, I glued foam pieces together vertically as terrain contours.

On the other part of my layout, in the corner where the track disappears into the hidden staging below Daneville, the terrain is more hilly. For the terrain here, I stacked foam pieces horizontally as well as aligning them side by side.

The scene in that corner is rather deep, so I made a part of the subterrain as a removable section for easier access while I worked on that section. My plan was to permanently attach the removable section after the scenery was completed.

In the corner where the track disappears into the staging below Daneville, the entrance is hidden with a tunnel. Before attaching the tunnel portal permanently, I tested the clearance by running a consist of my longest and tallest cars through it. For more on constructing the tunnel portal, see page 80.

Making a liftout section for better access

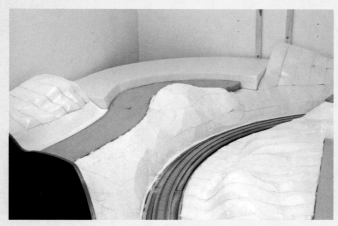

1. I started by cutting out a base layer for the removable section from a foam sheet. The section should fit between the backdrop and the road, which is an odd shape.

2. I glued a couple of foam blocks to the base. I used the sandwich method here, but gluing foam terrain contours together vertically would also work.

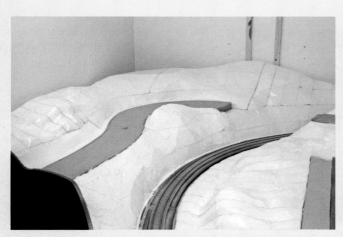

3. Like shaping a sculpture, I cut out the terrain contours from the foam blocks and sanded them smooth.

4. When the section is removed, it provides easy access for working on the scenery in the far corner of the scene.

STREETS AND HIGHWAYS

My model railroad is designed from a rail-fan's perspective. Roads have taken me to all my railroad adventures, so next to the track, roads have the highest priority on my layout. Roads are wonderful scenic elements. I use roads to cut through the scenery and create viewing lines and scene dividers.

The widest road on my layout is the main street in Daneville. This three-lane street is almost 14 feet long. The high-ways are all two lane. One of them goes on a bridge over the top of the track at the west end of Daneville, which creates a great scene divider. Another runs parallel with the railroad for more than 22 feet before it crosses the track and disappears in the distance. The narrow-est roads on my layout are the railroad's service roads. These dirt roads run along almost every inch of mainline railroad track.

I prefer to finish my roads completely before I begin to apply any scenery materials. Then you don't have to worry about getting the scenery dirty with sanding dust or spilling paint on it.

I try to keep my roads in prototypically correct width if I have the available space for it. My two-lane highways are 24–26 scale feet wide, which is close to proto-typical width. I know this takes up space, but a too-narrow road just doesn't look realistic to me.

The main street in Daneville is, as I mentioned earlier, the widest road on my layout. The space in Daneville only al-lows for three lanes, but even though the main street probably should have had at least four lanes to be more prototypi-cally correct, it still gives the feeling of a wide street. I have never had any visitors complain about the main street in Dane-ville being too narrow. On the contrary, I have had people ask why I wasted so much space on a street instead of having one or two more tracks for the trains.

Cross section of road

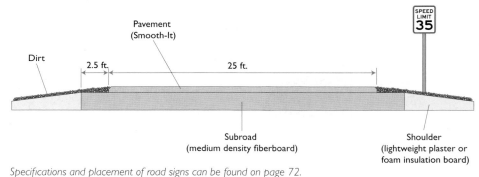

Specifications and placement of road signs can be found on page 72.

Installing the main street in Daneville

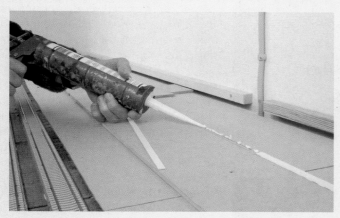

1. I glued .040"-thick plastic strips along the side of the street where all the buildings are located. I used a common all-purpose glue from the local building supply store.

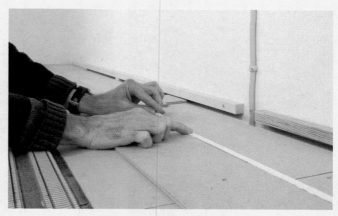

2. I pressed the strips in the glue, making sure that they were perfectly level. The sidewalks in front of the Daneville buildings will rest on the plastic strips when they are installed later.

3. On the other side of the road, I applied Woodland Scenics Paving Tape along the outside edge of the street. Paving Tape is a foam tape approximately .040" thick.

4. I mixed Smooth-It with water in a bowl. I stirred it carefully until there were no clumps left and poured the plaster on the road. Don't stir too hard because that will create a lot of air bubbles in the mix.

5. I spread the plaster evenly with a piece of styrene. After a few minutes, when the plaster set, I applied a thinner second layer of Smooth-It on top of the first.

6. After several days, when the plaster had dried completely, I removed the foam tape and sanded the surface. A power sander is very effective. I learned that you have to move the sander constantly and never sand the same area for more than a few seconds or else you risk sanding away all of the plaster.

On roads that had steep grades, I used a thicker mix of plaster than I used for more level roads. Before I applied the plaster, I wet the dry plaster where the streets joined to prevent the dry plaster from sucking all the moisture out of the wet plaster when it was applied.

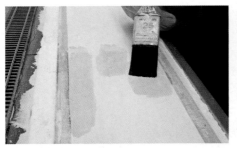
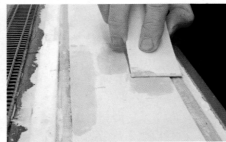

Sometimes the sanding revealed small holes caused by air bubbles. To repair these holes, I first wet these areas and then filled the holes with a little plaster using a piece of styrene to smooth out the repairs. After the repaired areas were dry, I sanded them lightly.

The roads needed to be trimmed at the grade crossings, and it is best to do this before the road is painted. With a sharp knife, I cut away excess plaster using a steel ruler as a guide.

I checked the space with one of the grade crossing pieces and trimmed off a little more of the plaster where it was too tight.

The explanation is simple. The main street, with its restaurants and hotels, is an important scenic element on my layout that makes the entire scene look more realistic than if I had added extra tracks instead.

Paving the roads

My highways and streets consist of a sub-road and a road surface. As described in the previous chapter, I made the subroads of ¼" MDF (medium density fiberboard). The ¼" MDF is relatively rigid, but it can be shaped, so you can create hills and dips in the road. To better simulate the paving, I applied a layer of plaster on top of the MDF. I used Woodland Scenics Smooth-It for the pavement, which is easy to work with, but you can use other types of plaster as well.

I make my subroads wider than the paved area, so there is space for laying paving tape along each edge of the road. Woodland Scenics Paving Tape is a foam tape approximately .040" thick. The area between the masking is filled with plaster. I spread the plaster evenly and let it set, not completely dry, before I apply a thin second layer.

When the plaster is completely dry, I remove the paving tape. I sand the road surface smooth with fine-grit sandpaper. I had quite a lot of road to sand, so to speed up the process I used my power sander. The power sander was indeed very effective, and I learned that you have to move the sander constantly and never sand the same area for more than a few seconds or all the plaster will be sanded

Making side streets

1. Apply foam tape along the outside edges of the side street.

2. Wet the main street with water where the side street joins. The water will prevent the dry plaster from absorbing moisture from the wet plaster and make it easier to create a smooth joint between the two streets.

3. Fill the area with plaster and let it dry before sanding the road surface.

away. I also sanded the sharp edges of the road by hand until they were slightly beveled.

In some places, the sanding revealed small holes in the surface caused by air bubbles from pouring the plaster. To repair these holes, I first wet the areas, filled the holes with a little plaster, and used a piece of styrene to smooth out the repairs. After the repaired areas were dry, I sanded them lightly.

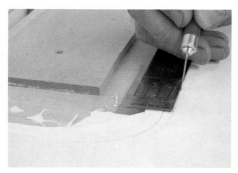

To mark the concrete curbs on the main street, I made a little groove 1/3" from the edge of the sidewalk's location.

I painted my roads with a 50/50 mix of Humbrol 140 Gray and 148 Random Tan. I gave the road two coats of paint. When the paint soaks down into the plaster, it will leave a realistic-looking surface that is not completely even-colored.

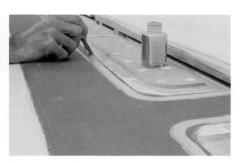

On the main street, I masked the outside edge of the curbs with masking tape and painted them in a concrete color mixed from equal amounts of Model Master 1730 Flat Gull Gray, 1706 Sand, and 1768 Flat White.

Adding a parking lot for the yard office

1. The parking lot at the yard office is made the same way as the highways. Using foam tape, I masked the outside edge, which butted up to the office foundation (made from sheet styrene). I then filled the remaining area with plaster and smoothed it out.

2. Parking lots are often not as well maintained as highways, so I only gave the parking lot a single layer of plaster since I wanted the surface to have a more irregular look than the roads.

3. After removing the foam tape, I sanded the surface lightly and gave it one coat of a warm gray paint because I didn't want it to look too uniform.

4. In this photo of the final result, you can see how the paint was absorbed in the plaster randomly, which gives it a very realistic "old asphalt" look.

The curbs on the main street in Daneville were painted in the same concrete color as the styrene sidewalks. Note the unevenly colored surface of the street, which is accomplished by giving the surface only two coats of gray. Giving it three or more coats would have resulted in a completely even gray surface that would have looked less realistic.

To ensure that all turn arrows were completely identical, I first made a template from a piece of cardboard.

Using the template as a guide, I drew the contour of the turn arrow on a piece of masking tape.

Using a sharp knife, I cut out the arrows. Cutting the masking tape on a glass plate made it an easy task.

Painting the roads

You can paint the plaster with either acrylic or enamel colors. I use Humbrol or Model Master enamel paint for my roads and apply it with a brush. Enamel colors seem to soak into the surface better than acrylics and dry with a flatter finish.

It requires several layers of paint to create an even and uniformly colored surface, but a completely uniform surface it is not always desirable. A less uniformly colored surface can, in many cases, look more realistic then a completely uniform one. New pavement requires at least three coats of paint. For slightly older pavement, I give the plaster two coats, and to produce very old pavement, I apply only a single coat of paint. I gave most of the highways on my layout two coats of paint.

Finishing Main Street

1. I started with painting the white stop line and pedestrian crossings. I masked the outlines with masking tape and rubbed the edges of the tape to prevent paint from creeping under it.

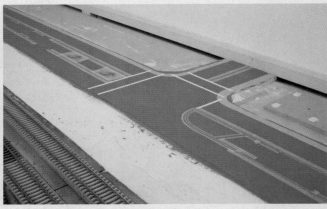

2. I cut out masks for the turn arrows from pieces of wide masking tape and applied them to the road. I also masked the rest of the road striping.

3. I painted the turn arrows white and most of the road striping yellow.

4. With a sponge, I applied some black powdered chalk down the center of each lane. I did not seal the powder with varnish.

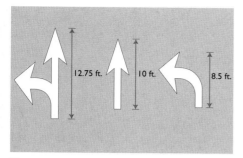
These are proportions for various turn arrows.

Applying striping and markings

I brush-paint all striping and markings on my roads. My hand is not steady enough to do it freehand, so I first mask the outside edges of the stripes with masking tape before I paint the striping and markings. Always rub the edges of the tape to

I don't bother masking the ends of the broken center lines, only the sides. I painted the stripes yellow and removed the tape after the paint had dried.

Paint formulas for roads

Concrete:
Equal amounts of Model Master
1730 Flat Gull Gray
1706 Sand
1768 Flat White

Asphalt:
Equal amounts of Humbrol
140 Gray
148 Random Tan

Striping and weathering highways

1. The highways received two coats of warm gray paint. When the paint dried, I masked the outside edges of the double yellow center line. I rubbed the edges of the tape to keep paint from creeping under it.

2. I filled the area with yellow Humbrol paint. One coat does not cover completely, but I leave it like that because the random coverage looks realistic. Real road stripes don't look completely uniform unless they have just been painted.

3. Be careful when you remove the masking tape so it does not take bits of the gray paint with it. The best way to remove the tape is to slowly pull it off at a backward angle.

4. The white stripes seen along the edges of major highways were painted the same way as the center stripes.

5. With a sponge, I applied some black powdered chalk down the center of each lane. Be careful not to apply too much powder. I always wipe off the sponge on a sheet of paper before dipping it in the powder.

6. Finally, I gave the edges of the highways a light spray of sand color to help them blend in with the surrounding scenery, which will be applied later.

Marking roads at a grade crossing

1. I made drawings for the road markings on my computer and printed them out on paper. I glued the paper to a piece of masking tape, and with a sharp knife, I cut out masks for the Rs.

2. I glued the print of the big X to a piece of cardboard and cut out the X. Using the cardboard template as a guide, I drew contours of the X on the road.

3. I masked the outlines of the X and the wide stripes at each end with masking tape. I also added the two Rs that I cut out earlier.

4. I filled the masked areas with white paint and let them dry before removing the masking tape.

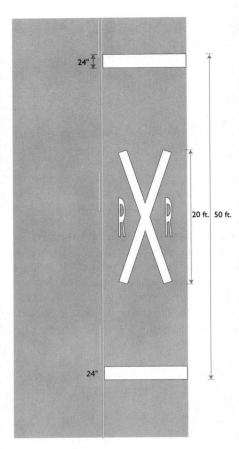

These are the proportions for grade crossing road markings.

This view shows Highway 41 running along the railroad track all the way to Daneville.

This photo shows an overview of the various types of pavement. To the left is Highway 41 and to the right, Daneville's main street. The parking lot at the UP yard office is in the foreground.

prevent paint from creeping under it. I use Tamiya masking tape because it does not stick as much to the surface and is easy to remove without taking bits of the road paint with it.

More complex road markings such as railroad crossing markings require a little preparation. I made the drawings for them on my computer and printed them out in the correct size. I used the prints to make templates for the masking.

Weathering

I weather my roads with black powdered chalk followed by a light spray of a sand color along the edge of the road. The powdered chalk adheres very well to the roads' flat surface, so a sealing coat of flat varnish is not required. I prefer to finish my roads completely, including weathering, before I apply any ground cover to the surrounding terrain.

Roadside details, such as signs and highway guardrails, give your roads a more authentic look. I normally add highway guardrails before I apply any scenery because you need to drill a lot of mounting holes for them, and it is easier to mark exactly where to drill on an unscenicked surface.

This picture shows Highway 51 going over the top of the track and turning into Daneville's main street.

The highway on the other part of my layout is the only road that received three coats of gray paint to represent a newly paved road.

I placed highway guardrails where they were necessary. The guardrails are from Rix products. After assembling the sections, I painted them with Model Master Light Ghost Gray. I then dusted them with a lighter gray (Cam Gray) to give them a weathered look.

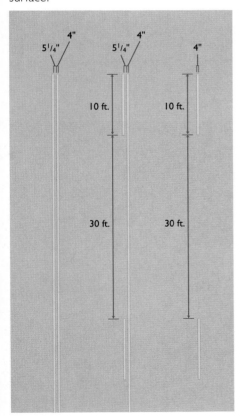

These are the dimensions and spacing I used for my road striping.

Inspired by a picture I took of historic Route 66, I painted cracks in the paving on part of Highway 41 using a dark gray thinned with approximately 50 percent thinner.

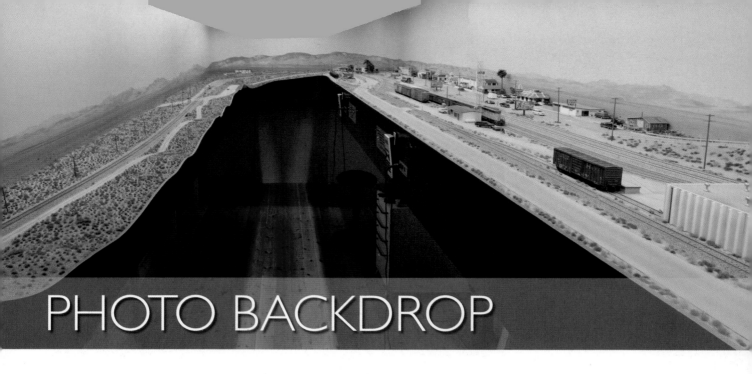

PHOTO BACKDROP

To many modelers, painting a backdrop is a source of frustration, and it is to me as well. I have painted backdrops for my two previous layouts and have always found it difficult to find the right balance between not making them too detailed or being too sketchy. A well-done backdrop should not really be noticed. I have seen beautifully painted backdrops, real pieces of art, but you often start studying the painting rather than looking at the layout. On the other hand, you don't want your backdrop to look too simple either because that can be distracting as well.

I needed two backdrops for my new layout, one for the Daneville area and one behind the cement plant. The Daneville backdrop measured 45 feet and the cement plant backdrop was 22 feet long. (Both were 30" high.)

The big decision used to be whether to use acrylic or oil paint for your backdrop, but thanks to the digital revolution another option has emerged: the photographic backdrop. Nowadays, most of us have everything needed to create artwork for a photographic backdrop, including a digital camera, a computer, and a photo enhancement program such as Adobe Photoshop, which I used.

The same general rule applies for creating a photographic backdrop as it does for a painted one. Avoid too many details and odd elements that can catch a viewer's attention. One way to do this is by making the backdrop from numerous images—painting with pictures, you could say. I had to do that anyway as no single photo would be wide enough to cover all 45 feet of the Daneville backdrop.

The first task was to find the pictures for it, so I went to Southern California, the locale for my fictitious railroad, to shoot distant mountain ranges and desert scenery. I took all the photos between noon and early afternoon, when the sun was high in the sky, so I didn't have to worry about conflicting shadows when I made the backdrop. I took plenty of pictures to be sure to have enough to work with.

After returning, I selected the images I wanted for my backdrop. I used 20 different photos to create the artwork for the backdrop. I started by making sub-images that I later combined into one big panoramic image consisting of several layers. When I was pleased with how all the elements were located and how they blended together, I didn't need the layers any more, so I saved a copy as a TIFF file without preserving the layers.

I adjusted the colors in the file. Because the images were all pictures of distant objects, their colors were relatively muted. To make the photos match the model scenery better, I increased the saturation (intensity of the colors) and the contrast.

I also took out much of the blue in the mountain ranges.

I had the image printed out at a place that makes posters for exhibitions. Before I had the entire 45 feet printed out, I had a small section printed out to test the colors with my layout. It turned out to be a good idea. Even though I had taken out a lot of blue, the first test print still appeared too blue. Photos of distant objects will always contain a lot of blue. It is also a good idea to check that none of the fore-

The prints were applied to flexible boards that I attached to wood strips on the wall with small nails.

Layer 3: distant mountain

These five photos make up the distant mountain range. I stacked the pictures in separate layers in the same document and aligned them to one long photo. You can either do this using Auto Align Layers and Auto Blend Layers in Photoshop or by manually placing the images in separate layers and blending them together with soft layer masks where they overlap as described in layer 2. Merge the stack of pictures to one single layer and extract the mountain from the photo, copy it, open the work document, and paste the mountain image in a separate layer in the work document (layer 3).

The easiest way of extracting the mountain from the background is with the Extract filter in Photoshop. Unfortunately, it was eliminated from Photoshop CS5, so it is only available in earlier versions of Photoshop. The Extract filter provides a quick way to isolate a foreground object and erase its background. Even objects with irregular or undefinable edges are easily clipped from their backgrounds with a minimum of manual work. There are other ways of extracting an object. In many cases, you can use the Magic Wand tool, or you can do it manually by drawing a clipping path.

I softened the lower edge of the mountain using a layer mask. I painted a soft mask using the Airbrush tool. The soft edge helps the mountain blend in seamlessly with the background it is placed on. I needed two distant mountains, so I used the same image twice on the backdrop.

Only layer 3 is visible.

Sky layer (1), desert layer (2), and distant mountain layer (3) are visible.

Layers 1, 2, and 3 are visible.

Layer 4: middle range mountain

The mountain range for the middle area of the backdrop consists of this series of eight pictures.

I followed the same procedure as on the distant mountain by aligning and merging the images to one long mountain range.

Only layer 4 is visible.

I extracted the mountain, placed it in the work document, and softened the lower edge as I did with the distant mountain.

Sky layer (1), desert layer (2), distant mountain layer (3), and middle ground mountain layer (4) are visible.

Note how the mountains blend beautifully in with the desert due to the soft layer masks.

Layers 1, 2, 3, and 4 are visible.

Layer 5: foreground mountain

The fifth and final layer is a little mountain in the foreground at the right. These two images create the foreground mountain. I used the same procedure as with the two previous mountains by aligning and merging the images into one. I removed the telephone poles in the foreground by using the Clone tool.

Only layer 5 is visible.

As on the previous layers, I extracted the mountain before copying and pasting it in my work document. I also softened the lower edge the same way as with the other mountains.

Sky layer (1), desert layer (2), distant mountain layer (3), middle ground mountain layer (4), and foreground mountain layer (5) are visible. This completes the basic artwork for the backdrop. I adjusted the colors and saved a copy of the artwork as a TIFF file without preserving the layers.

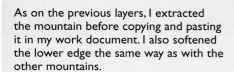

Layers 1, 2, 3, 4, and 5 are visible.

BALLAST & GROUND COVER

With the backdrop in place, I could proceed with the scenery. Now it was time to cover the terrain with dirt, weeds, and brush. This is the fun part—where you transform your foam terrain into a realistic-looking landscape.

The choice of colors is essential for creating realistic-looking scenery. I model the Southern Californian desert, and to capture the look of a hot, dry desert, you have to stay within a relatively limited range of brown, yellow, and olive green shades of color.

I did some research regarding the colors of the soil in the Mojave Desert. On a trip to California, I collected dirt samples from three different areas of the Mojave Desert. When I compared the samples, it turned out that the color of the dirt was different in all three places, ranging from a light gray-beige to a warm brown-gray. I picked the brown-gray as the color I wanted for the desert soil on my layout. I sifted the Mo-

jave soil for use on the layout and ended up with two different grain sizes: fine and coarse. I used the coarse soil as rubble and small rocks.

When I studied the Mojave soil samples under the layout's lighting, the soil appeared darker than it did under bright sunlight. I therefore combined the Mojave dirt with Low Desert Soil from Arizona Rock &

Yours truly collecting dirt samples in the middle of the Mojave Desert. Photo by Ken Perry

Mineral, which is a much lighter shade than the original Mojave dirt. I ended up using a mix with a ratio of one part Mojave dirt to three parts Low Desert Soil, and it looked pretty close to the real thing when viewed under the layout's lighting conditions.

The colors of all the other scenery materials on my layout were chosen to match the color of the soil.

First things first

The first scenery elements I added were some rock outcroppings in a few locations. I started by making a selection of rock castings in various sizes. I filled rubber rock molds with Lightweight Hydrocal from Woodland Scenics. When the castings dried, I removed them from the molds and colored them with stains made from Woodland Scenics Earth Colors Liquid Pigments. I gave them a warm grayish-brown color that matched the color of the surrounding desert soil.

Coloring my rock castings to match the color of the surrounding soil helped integrate the rocks in the scene in a more realistic way.

Next, before applying any ground cover to the layout, I added a selection of telephone poles. (For how to make the telephone poles, see page 70.) It was easier to insert the poles now because I could clearly see the exact location of each pole that I marked on the terrain without being obscured by scenery materials.

Applying ground cover

Before applying any ground cover, I first apply a base layer of dirt to the entire area. You do not have to use expensive scenery materials for the base layer. You can use any type of sand or dirt as it will be covered later with a top layer of desert soil. The purpose of this base layer is to create a coarse surface to help hold the final layer of desert soil and prevent it from being flushed away when you wet and glue it.

I brushed the terrain with thinned white glue and sprinkled it with a base layer of ground cover and let it dry for a couple of days. I then sprinkled the scene with desert soil. On flat terrain, I cover the entire area with dirt before I wet and glue it. On slopes and hilly terrain, I apply dirt to a small area at a time and soak it with water with some rubbing alcohol added to it. Then I go over the area again, but this time with white glue thinned with water.

I am often asked what ratio between water and alcohol and what ratio between glue and water to use. I don't use specific ratios but for the water–alcohol mix I use at least three times more water than alcohol. The water–white glue mix is about the same. You can also use Woodland Scenics Scenic Cement, which is a ready-to-use glue for ground cover and ballast, but I have found that, when using Scenic Cement, ground cover looks darker after it dries than it does when using white glue, so you have to take that into consideration when using Scenic Cement.

Ballasting the track

I do not ballast my track as a separate process. I apply ground cover and ballast in the same workflow. That way I don't have to go

Mixing ratios for ballast

Mainline track:
Equal amounts of
Arizona Rock & Mineral 130-2 NP Medium Gray and 138-2 CSX/SP

Secondary track:
Equal amounts of
Arizona Rock & Mineral 130-2 NP Medium Gray and ASOA 1710 Gneisschotter

Casting and coloring rocks

1. I mixed Lightweight Hydrocal from Woodland Scenics with water and poured the mix into the rock molds. It is a good idea to poke a stick in the wet plaster to release any air bubbles.

2. When the plaster had set for 30 minutes, I removed the castings from the molds by pressing gently on the back side of the rubber mold until the casting popped up.

3. I prepared stains in four different earth colors (Stone Gray, Black, Burnt Umber, and Yellow Ochre). I wet the casting before I applied the colors. I randomly dabbed the different colors on the castings.

Attaching rock castings to the terrain is easily done with a few dabs of lightweight filler applied on the back of the casting and then gently pressed in place.

Planting telephone poles

1. I marked locations for the poles with an A or a B, alternating the letters. Daneville is built on medium density fiberboard, so I drilled holes for the mounting pins needed on the poles and spaced them 12" apart.

2. I planted a pole in each hole using a small dab of glue. There is a pattern to the way the poles face. Every other pole faces the same direction, so a B pole is a mirror image of an A pole.

3. On the foam insulation terrain, I simply poked a hole in the foam with a screwdriver for each pole.

4. I planted the poles in the holes. As they fit tightly, I didn't have to glue the poles to the terrain.

over the same scene again and again. Not only does this save time, but the various elements also blend together nicely and provide realistic-looking results.

I use different colors of ballast depending on whether it represents new ballast or old ballast. For the main line, I mixed two gray shades of ballast. For secondary track, I used a more brownish mix.

Weeds and bushes

It has always been a challenge for me to model a convincing desert scene. The biggest challenge is how to make a 20"-deep scene look like a vast desert. A backdrop plays an important role, and it requires that the scene blends together with the backdrop extremely well. That makes modeling a desert more challenging than making a scene with trees or mountains, where you can more easily hide the transition between the modeled scene and the backdrop.

To many people, a desert is a vast area covered with dirt (or sand) and a sparse amount of shrubs and bushes. That is true in some areas, but I model the Mojave Desert

I used MiniNatur grass tufts for my desert scene. From a large selection of colors, I picked four shades that looked very desert-like: Long Tufts Early Fall, Long Tufts Late Fall, Two Color Grass Early Fall, and Two Color Grass Late Fall.

Applying ground cover around rock outcroppings

1. I brushed thinned white glue on the terrain around the rock outcroppings.

2. I placed some soil on a piece of paper and blew it onto the wet glue. Blow gently or you will blow soil back into your face.

3. I then brushed thinned white glue on the more-level terrain above the rocks.

4. I covered the wet glue with a layer of dirt.

5. With a homemade shaker jar, I applied a second layer of desert soil to the area.

6. Next, I applied talus to the slopes. After sprinkling it on with a spoon, I pushed the talus gently into the dirt with my finger.

7. I wet the area with a water and rubbing alcohol mix.

8. I placed some grass tufts on the wet soil.

9. Finally, I drizzled the area with thinned white glue and left it to dry.

Applying ground cover to the Daneville section

1. Applying ground cover and ballast to the entire Daneville area was done in the same workflow over a weekend. Buildings, telephone poles, and billboards were set into the scene first.

2. I started with the highway overpass at the west end of Daneville. I first brushed the slopes with thinned white glue.

3. I then sprinkled soil on the wet glue, working in small areas. If you work in a larger area, the glue will run to the bottom of the slope before you have time to cover it with soil.

4. When the entire slope was covered with dirt, I wet it with a mix of water and rubbing alcohol.

5. I applied a second layer of soil on top of the first. Applying a double layer ensures that the slope is properly covered with dirt.

6. I carefully dripped white glue thinned with water over the slope as to not wash the dirt down the slope.

7. I sprinkled a little more dirt on spots where the layer appeared too thin.

8. I then covered the area between the tracks and the main street.

9. With a soft brush, I wiped the street clean of dirt.

10. I drizzled the dirt with the water-alcohol mix.

11. I went over the area again but this time with thinned white glue.

12. While the glue was still wet, I applied a little yellow fiber grass here and there on top of the soil.

13. I continued on the other side of the track by first sprinkling soil on the area and then ballasting the tracks.

14. I wet the entire area, ballast and soil, with the water and alcohol mix.

15. I then dripped thinned white glue over the area. I started with the ballast and then applied it to the soil.

16. Right after applying the glue, I created a dirt road by sifting extra-fine dirt along the tracks.

17. I sprinkled a little yellow fiber grass along each side of the dirt road.

18. After several days, when the glue was completely dry, I rubbed the road with a stiff brush to add tire marks.

in Southern California, and most of it is actually overgrown with shrubs and small bushes.

I am constantly looking for scenery materials that I can use to make better-looking scenes. For my desert scene, I used Silhouette's (a German company) MiniNatur scenery materials. One series of grass tufts is well suited for desert shrubs, and the fall colors looked very desert-like, and they also matched the colors on my backdrop. I used four different colors of tufts for my desert scene. I also used a fiber mesh called Horse Tail that I cut into small pieces and used as scattered desert bushes.

I experimented with spreading the tufts on the dry dirt and then wet and glued everything in the same workflow. Unfortunately, this process didn't work well. Most of the tufts were still loose after the glue had dried, so there was no other alternative but to apply the tufts

The finished Daneville scene looking west.

The finished Daneville scene looking east.

Adding ballast to a turnout

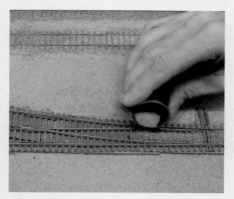

1. Applying ballast to a turnout, especially the areas with moving parts, requires that you be more careful than when ballasting regular track. I started by applying ballast between the ties below the switch point section.

2. With a fine, soft brush, I carefully wiped all ballast off the top of the ties. Any ballast remaining here will prevent the switch points from moving freely. You also have to be very careful that no ballast goes between the throw bar and the ties.

3. After the switch point section was done, I applied ballast to the rest of the turnout. I spread it evenly between the rails with a wide, soft brush.

4. I then sprinkled ballast on the edges of the turnout, being careful in the area around the throw bar.

5. With my soft brush, I wiped the top of the tie ends clean of ballast.

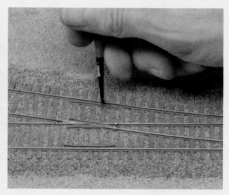

6. I removed ballast stuck between the guard rails and the stock rails with a fine brush.

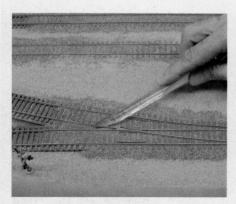

7. Finally, I tapped all the rails with the shaft of my brush to knock off the remaing ballast pieces from the top of the ties.

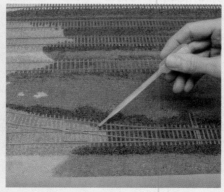

8. I soaked the ballast with the water and rubbing alcohol mix. I not only soaked the turnouts but the entire area.

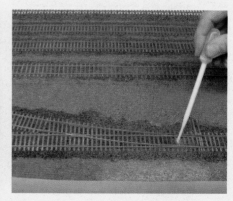

9. I then dripped thinned white glue on the wet ballast. Drip the glue carefully at the switch point area, so you don't wash any ballast up on the top of the ties.

Creating a desert scene

1. I first brushed the terrain with thinned white glue. I applied glue to one 2-foot section at a time.

2. I then sprinkled a base layer of dirt on the wet glue. This base layer creates an adhering surface for the top layer of desert dirt and prevents it from being flushed away when you wet and glue it.

3. When the base layer was dry, I applied the top layer of desert soil. I use a home-made shaker for sprinkling the dirt evenly on the area.

4. To protect delicate areas, such as the movable parts on turnouts, I covered them with a piece of cardboard before I applied the ground cover. I also covered the road with cardboard.

5. I then applied ballast to the track. I tried to apply it as evenly as possible. For better control of the flow, I used a small film container for applying ballast.

6. I spread the ballast evenly with a wide, soft brush. I tapped the rails with the shaft of my brush to knock off any remaining ballast from the top of the ties.

7. When the entire area was covered with soil and ballast, I wet it with water and a little rubbing alcohol. I worked in 2–3 foot sections at a time.

8. Then I went over the area again with white glue thinned with water. I repeated the process on each section until the entire scene was completed.

9. I placed tufts of all four colors on a sheet of cardboard. I picked the tufts randomly and applied them on the terrain with a dab of glue.

10. I used MiniNatur Horse Tail to create the scattered bushes. The colors I used were Early Fall and Late Fall.

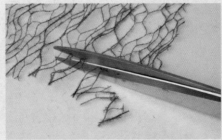

11. I cut out a small piece of the material with a pair of scissors and folded it into a bush.

12. I then made a hole in the foam and planted the bush in it with a dab of glue.

Making a railroad service road

1. The dirt roads were made in the same workflow as when the rest of the ground cover and ballast were applied. I first wet the area and then applied thinned white glue.

2. Immediately after the glue was applied, I sprinkled a topcoat of very fine grained desert soil on the service road.

3. When the glued area was completely dry, after several days, I created tire marks by rubbing the surface with a stiff brush. You can also use the tip of your finger or a sanding stick.

4. The finished area as it looked after the weeds and shrubs were added.

The completed desert scene as it looks from a birds-eye view.

one by one, with a dab of glue, to my 25-square-foot desert scene. What I thought would be a tedious process actually went quicker than I expected. I could cover approximately 2 square feet in an hour, so it was possible to do the entire desert scene in less than two days. I have to confess that I didn't do it in two days. To make the task less tedious, I worked an hour each day until the area was covered with tufts.

To make things go faster, I made a tufts palette. I took an assortment of the four colors of tufts, peeled off the backing paper, and placed them on a sheet of cardboard. I then randomly picked the tufts from the palette one by one, applied a dab of white glue under them, and placed them on the terrain.

GRADE CROSSINGS

The crossing gates from NJ International are non-operational, but they can be fairly easily modified to be operational.

I didn't like the cast warning lights on the crossing gates, so I snapped them off and made new ones out of small pieces of flat brass bar and red lenses from MV Products.

Outside Daneville, the old highway crosses the main line. If a train approaches, motorists will be warned by flashing cantilever crossing signals and operating gates. I used products from various manufacturers to create an operating grade crossing. The cantilever crossing signals are from Walthers, and the gates are from NJ International. The gates are operated by a Tortoise switch machine. Everything is controlled by a circuit from Logic Rail Technologies called Grade Crossing Pro.

The NJ International crossing gates are nonoperational, but they are easily modified to be operational. To do so, attach a wire at the counterweight and connect the other end of the wire to an operating gate mechanism mounted under the grade crossing.

I have several BLMA Models concrete grade crossings on my layout. The pieces are cast in light gray styrene to make them look like concrete, but to obtain a more-realistic look, I painted them with my own concrete blend of Model Master Flat Gull Gray, Sand, and Flat White in equal proportions. The grade crossing concrete slabs have a metal frame around the edges that prevents the concrete edges from cracking under the weight of crossing vehicles. On brand new grade crossings, the metal will have an orange color due to a protective coating, but after awhile, the orange wears off, and the

The grade crossing is triggered by photo cells placed in the middle of the track between the ties. If you don't always run your layout fully illuminated, Logic Rail Technologies also offers the Grade Crossing Pro system with infrared sensors.

Making a gate crossing mechanism

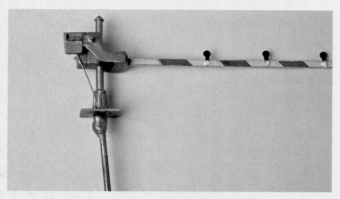

1. I drilled one hole in the gate's counterweight and another through the base for the wire. I then soldered a piece of brass tube to the underside of the base where the hole is. The brass tube serves as a guide for the wire. I slid a thin piano wire through the brass tube and connected the end to the counterweight by bending it at a 90 degree angle.

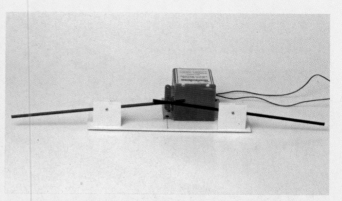

2. The gates are operated by a Tortoise switch machine. The motion arms are square carbon fiber tubes, which are very rigid, and the support brackets are made from .080" (2mm) styrene. The gate mechanism is mounted under the grade crossing, and the wires from the gates are connected to the motion arms.

3. The slots in the motion arms make sure that the pin from the switch machine can move smoothly.

4. The motion arms are attached to the support brackets with a small screw. I placed spacers between the bracket sides, so the arms could move freely.

metal edge appears brownish. I painted these edges brown, and gave the concrete slabs a wash to make them appear older.

I removed ballast from the top of the ties and then inserted the concrete slabs, checking that none of the pieces were higher than the rails. I glued them with white glue but cyanoacrylate adhesive will also work fine.

I also have a couple of secondary grade crossings on my layout. They are scratch-built from .0416" × .0625" basswood. I cut strips in appropriate lengths and glued them to a .010" styrene base, which makes the parts easier to mount on the layout later. I aged the wood with a stain of Vallejo 042 Camouflage Black Brown.

This view of the finished grade crossing shows the weathered crossing, gates, and signals.

Painting and weathering concrete gate crossings

1. I wanted to paint and weather the modern grade crossings from BLMA Models on my layout. The plastic concrete slabs come as pairs, and I separated them so I had individual slabs just like the real thing.

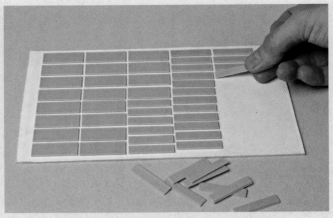

2. To prevent the parts from being blown away during the airbrushing, I attached them to a sheet of self-adhesive paper glued to a piece of cardboard.

3. I sprayed the pieces a concrete gray color mixed from equal amounts of Model Master Flat Gull Gray, Sand, and Flat White.

4. I brush-painted the metal edge that frames each concrete slab. I masked along the two long sides with tape and painted the metal edges a brownish color.

5. Then I masked the short sides and painted them.

6. I put the pieces back on the self-adhesive paper and gave them all a dark gray wash to weather them like old concrete.

Making a wood gate crossing

1. Secondary railroad crossings on my layout are made from wood. I cut strips of .0416" x .0625" basswood in appropriate lengths. I also cut bases for the wood strips from a .010" styrene sheet.

2. On the wood strips aligned along the outside edge of the rails, I made a cutout, so they would fit over the rail spikes.

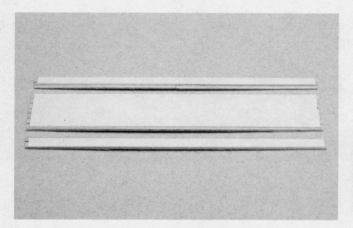

3. I glued all the wood pieces to the styrene bases with a drop of cyanoacrylate adhesive.

4. I drilled a series of small holes in the wood strips to simulate the holes for the countersunk bolts used on these wood grade crossings.

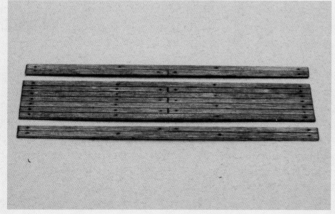

5. I stained the wood with Vallejo 042 Camouflage Black Brown to age it.

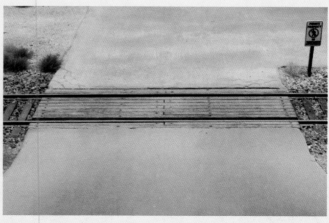

6. I wiped the top of the ties to remove ballast and then glued the grade crossing parts in place. Make sure that the wood is not higher than the rails in any place.

TELEPHONE POLES

A string of telephone poles along the railroad track will improve the looks of any scene on a model railroad.

I had saved all the telephone poles from my old layout, and my plan was to reuse them on the new layout, but when I looked closer at them, they didn't look as good as I remembered. The poles lacked a true wooden look and didn't live up to my ambitions of building a better layout in every aspect, so I decided to make new telephone and utility poles for the entire layout. I was very pleased with the wooden look I gave the ties on my Micro Engineering flextrack and decided to use the same painting technique on the telephone poles.

I had plenty of Rix telephone pole kits on hand, so the first step was to figure out how many poles I needed. I made pencil marks on the layout where the poles should go. Then I wrote an A or a B alternately at each mark to indicate which type of pole should be placed there. There is a pattern to which way the poles

face. Every other pole faces in the same direction, so a B pole is a mirror image of an A pole. I maintained 12" spaces between the poles.

I recorded how many poles of each type and in which heights I needed. The poles are taller in populated areas where the lines have to go over highways and railroads than they are outside towns and in open country such as my desert where there is no population.

Before attaching the crossarms, I scraped all the poles with a razor saw to create a rough wood texture. I cut the crossarms from the sprue, and since I model modern times, I cut off some of the insulators. I also trimmed the top crossarms, so they were shorter than the lower crossarms. On the top crossarm, I snapped off all but two insulators.

I used both the clear and clear green Rix crossarms. After painting the arms, the clear insulators appear to be glass ones, as used on the prototype.

I glued the crossarms to the poles using ordinary liquid plastic cement. Finally, I drilled a hole in the bottom end of each pole and inserted a piece of brass wire to make it easier to plant the poles on the layout.

I painted all the poles a light gray color. I could not use an airbrush without masking the insulators, so I decided that it would be quicker to paint them by hand. I let the gray paint dry completely before I gave the poles a blackish-brown stain. The stain consisted of water with a several drops of Vallejo Cam Black Brown added to it. I also added a few drops of rubbing alcohol to the stain to make it flow better.

I added transformers to a few of the poles. I made them from styrene sprue and a piece of .020" styrene sheet.

As mentioned in the chapter on ballast and ground cover, I attached the telephone poles to the layout before I added any ground cover to the scenery. After finishing the scenery, I attached wires to the telephone poles. I used EZ Line from Berkshire Junction, which is an elastic string that can survive being bumped. I gave the lines a little slack, so they hang in a realistic way. I found that after a few weeks, the lines had contracted so most of the sagging was gone, so you need to compensate for that when you add the lines by letting them sag a little more than you had anticipated.

It can be troublesome having sagging lines. Even the slightest turbulence in the air will cause the wires to touch each other, and they tend to cling together when they touch. I had to tighten the wires between the poles closest to the entrance of my train room because every time the door opened, I had to separate the wires between the poles. The sagging wires look good as long as you don't sneeze.

After the scenery was completed, I attached wires to the telephone poles. I used EZ Line from Berkshire Junction. To make the lines look more realistic, I gave the lines a little slack, so they sagged a little.

I attached the wire to the insulators with a tiny dab of cyanoacrylate adhesive (CA) applied with a metal pin. Be very careful not to get any CA on the string except for the spot where it touches the insulator. CA will make the string curl.

Constructing telephone poles

1. I scraped the poles with a razor saw to roughen the poles' texture. Rub the pole with a toothbrush to get rid of all loose material.

2. Rix offer two versions of clear crossarms for their poles. This is a brilliant product. When you paint the crossarms, leave the insulators clear in order to produce glass insulators that were used on the prototype. I trimmed the upper crossarm and cut off some of the insulators to create a more modern look. I glued the crossarms to the poles using ordinary liquid plastic cement.

4. To finish, I first painted all the poles and crossarms in a light gray color.

5. After the paint was dry, I gave the poles and crossarms a coat of stain made from Vallejo Cam Black Brown, water, and a few drops of alcohol, which makes the stain flow better.

3. I added transformers to a few of the poles. I made the transformers from styrene sprue and a piece of .020" styrene sheet. The thin wires coming out of the transformers are brass wire. The copper springs attached to the top crossarm simulate strain insulators that connect to power lines.

6. I painted the braces gray, and the poles were ready to plant.

ROAD SIGNS

Little things like road signs can make a big difference in a scene. I have various types of signs along all the roads on my layout that include warning signs, regulatory signs, route signs, and town signs.

It is very easy to make your own road signs. All you need is a computer and a laser printer. You can photograph the real signs, print out the photos, and use them as printed. You can also use the photos as reference for creating your own signs with a computer, which is what I did. I created the artwork for my road signs in Adobe Illustrator and printed them out on self-adhesive paper. I attached the paper to a .010" styrene sheet and cut the signs out. I made posts for the signs from T-shaped styrene strips or stripwood. I glued the signs to their posts and painted the posts and backs of the signs light gray.

I poked holes in my foam with a screwdriver and planted the signs in the holes, securing them with a dab of glue.

Signs should stand no less than 5 scale feet above the road surface. I did not have the space to place my signs 12 feet from the edge of the road specified by government regulations, so I placed mine closer.

Sign sizes (in inches)

| | Conventional road | | Expressway | Freeway |
	Single lane	Multilane		
Stop sign	30 × 30	36 × 36	36 × 36	
Speed limit sign	24 × 30	30 × 36	36 × 48	48 × 60
Warning sign	30 × 30	36 × 36	36 × 36	36 × 36
Grade crossing warning sign	30" Dia.	30" Dia.		
Advisory speed plaque (under warning sign)	18 × 18	18 × 18	24 × 24	30 × 30
Route sign	24 × 24	24 × 24	24 × 24	24 × 24

Easy-to-make road signs

1. A selection of the road signs I made for my layout includes town signs, speed limit signs, route signs, warning signs, and a stop sign.

2. I sized and printed the signs on self-adhesive paper, which I glued to .010" styrene sheet, and then cut out the signs.

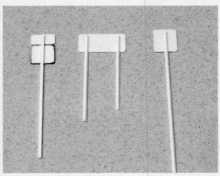

3. I glued the signs to posts made from T-shaped styrene strips or stripwood.

4. I painted the posts and the back sides of the signs light gray and planted them on my layout.

A pair of signs guards the grade crossing where the spur to the plastic pellet transfer facility crosses Highway 41.

I think all railfans are familiar with this kind of sign.

Warning signs for a sharp turn make the roads safer for the motorists in Daneville.

CONCRETE TRESTLE

Before I installed the bridge on my layout, I glued a piece of cork roadbed to the top of it with contact cement.

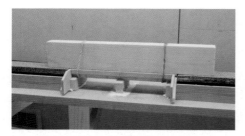

I attached the bridge with filler. To ensure that the bridge deck was flush with the roadbed, I attached a wood block to the top of the bridge with rubber bands and placed the bridge in the cutout. When the filler dried, I cut the rubber bands and removed the wood block.

It can be a stunning sight to watch a train roll over a huge railroad bridge, but the way I had designed my new layout did not offer much opportunity for impressive bridges. I had space for a more modest structure though. In the desert scene opposite Daneville, I installed a small trestle.

If you model, as I do, modern railroads, an obvious choice would be a kit of a modern concrete segmental bridge. I used one from Scale Segmental Bridge Co., but more are available from BLMA and other manufacturers. The pieces are made of plaster, which is a good material for creating realistic concrete. I used a T-girder Type 2 segmental bridge with round concrete pilings on the shelf. It required some trimming to fit my scene. The center support beam was too tall, so I trimmed about ³⁄₁₆" (5mm) from it with a razor saw. The round concrete pilings had to be shortened to ³⁄₈" (9mm).

The plaster castings are light gray and look like concrete right out of the box, but

a little weathering with a stain improved the look of the bridge. I made the stain by adding a few drops of black and Stone Gray (Woodland Scenics Earth Colors) to water, and gave the parts several washes. It is easier to stain the pieces before assembling them. Before applying the stain, I moistened the castings with clean water.

Let the pieces dry thoroughly before assembling the bridge. The glue will not bond if the parts are still damp. I used a cyanoacrylate adhesive gel to glue the pieces together. The glue bonds instantly, so you have to be precise when joining the pieces. When the parts are glued together, it is not easy to take them apart again without breaking them.

Installing the bridge

The bridge is a part of the subroadbed, so it is best to install the bridge when the subroadbed is in place and before you have laid track. I attached the bridge to the layout with plaster filler.

Building a trestle from a plaster kit

1. The plaster T-girder Type 2 segmental bridge kit consists of four span pieces, four pilings, two end walls, and one center support beam.

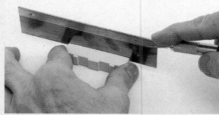

2. There is not much clearance under the bridge, so I trimmed about 3/16" off the center support beam with a razor saw to make it fit my scene.

3. I sanded the underside of the center beam smooth by rubbing it gently on a sheet of fine sandpaper.

4. All edges on the center beam are beveled, so I beveled the lower edges by rubbing the beam on the sandpaper at a 45 degree angle.

5. The round concrete pilings had to be shortened to 3/8". I just cut off the four pieces I needed from one of the pilings.

6. I gave the pieces a stain made from water and a few drops of black and Stone Gray Earth Colors from Woodland Scenics. For better coverage, I moistened the castings with clean water before applying the stain.

7. Let the pieces dry thoroughly before assembling the bridge. I used a gel-type cyanoacrylate adhesive to glue the pieces together.

8. I started by gluing 2 x 2 span pieces together, end to end. I aligned the pieces along a straightedge when I pushed them together.

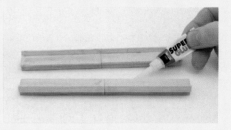

9. Be precise when joining the two span sides together as the glue bonds instantly.

10. Glue the end walls to the span section. Again, be sure the alignment is correct. When the glue bonds, it will not be easy to separate the pieces without damaging something.

11. I attached the short pilings to the center support beam with a drop of glue.

12. The last step is mounting the center support section. Before installing it on the layout, I weathered the assembled bridge lightly with black and brown powdered chalk.

HIGHWAY BRIDGE

At the west end of Daneville, there is a highway overpass where Highway 58 crosses over the tracks before it enters the city limits. This highway bridge is an important visual element on my layout. A highway overpass adds a vertical element to an otherwise flat desert layout. The overpass also covers the unrealistic sharp curve the track makes just before it enters Daneville.

My highway bridge crosses the track at a 45 degree angle. In the real world, where there is plenty of space, bridges are rarely modified, but due to limited space on my layout, I had to make my bridge in a diagonal shape. Fortunately, there is a prototype for everything, and I found a diagonal shaped bridge in Cajon Pass. I took pictures of it as proof if someone claims that a highway bridge can never be made that way in open country.

I used a Modern Highway Overpass kit from Rix Products. First, I glued three roadway sections together. The roadway was cut diagonally at a 45 degree angle at each end. I glued beam sections together and cut the ends diagonally to match the roadway. I also glued sections of guardrails together and trimmed them to the same length as the roadway. The guardrails were not cut at a 45 degree angle.

The center support beam had to be extended due to the diagonal design of the bridge. This was easily done by combining the parts from two beams.

Concrete bridges often have a slightly arched shape. As the beams and guardrails were completely straight and quite stiff, I had to come up with a way to give them an arched shape. I made a jig by gluing pieces of strip styrene on a piece

This highway bridge in Cajon Pass, Calif., is an example of a diagonally shaped bridge crossing the track at an angle.

Constructing a highway bridge

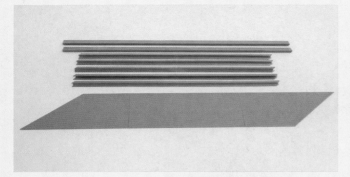

1. To begin, I glued the three Rix roadway sections together and made diagonal cuts at each end. I then glued sections of beams together and cut the ends at the same angle as the roadway. Next, I glued sections of guardrails together and trimmed them to the same length as the roadway but did not cut them diagonally.

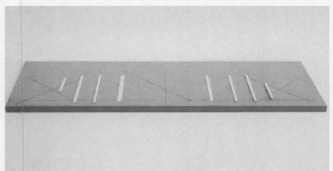

2. I made a jig consisting of styrene strips on a piece of MDF (medium density fiberboard). I glued small stacks of .040" styrene strips together in various heights. I then glued the stacks to the MDF with the tallest stacks towards the ends and the lowest in the middle. The purpose of the jig was to give the bridge a slightly arched shape.

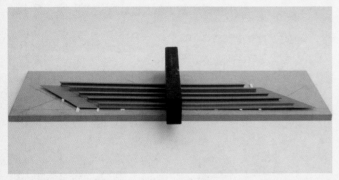

3. I placed the roadway face down and glued the five beams to it. I used a weight to force the roadway and beams down in the jig. After 24 hours of drying time, I glued the guardrails to the roadway and put it back in the jig, weighed it down, and let it dry for another 24 hours.

4. Because the support beam had to be positioned at a 45 degree angle, it had to be extended to span the roadway. I did that by combining the parts from two sets of support beams. The extended support has four posts instead of three.

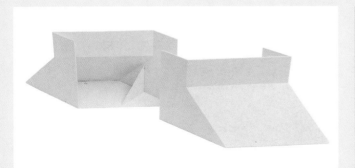

5. I made the two abutments from .040" sheet styrene, with an angle that matched the bridge's diagonal shape.

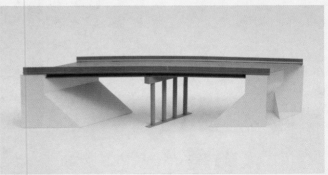

6. I attached the abutments and center support to the bridge and it was ready for painting and weathering.

Painting and weathering a highway bridge

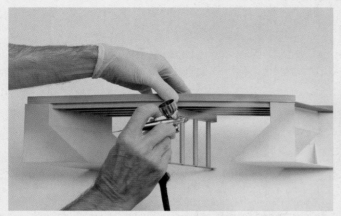

1. I gave the bridge several coats of my own concrete paint mixture, starting with the underside of the bridge.

2. I then gave the bridge several washes of a stain to give the evenly colored concrete surface a more uneven dirty look.

3. Then I applied the road striping. I masked the outline of the double yellow center line with masking tape and painted the line with a fine brush.

4. To finish, I weathered the bridge, using black and brown powdered chalk. Using a soft brush, I applied the chalk to the abutments, beams, and guardrails.

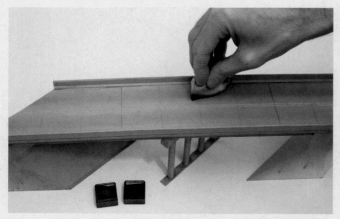

5. On the roadway, I used a sponge to smudge powder down the center of each lane. I didn't give the bridge a sealing coat of varnish as the powder adhered very well to the flat Model Master paint.

Paint formulas and ratios

Concrete color:
Equal amounts of Model Master
1730 Flat Gull Gray, 1706 Sand, and 1768 Flat White

An alternative is Vallejo 71045 US Light Gray which produces a warm concrete color.

Stain:
A 50/50 mix of Woodland Scenics C1220 Black and C1218 Stone Gray Liquid Pigments Earth Colors mixed with plenty of water and a few drops of rubbing alcohol

of medium density fiberboard, with the tallest strips toward the ends and the lower ones at the center. I laid the roadway facedown, glued the five beams to it, and placed heavy weights on top of it to press the roadway and beams down in the jig. I left it to dry for 24 hours before removing the weights. Then, I glued the guardrails to the roadway and put it back in the jig, weighed it down, and let it dry for another 24 hours before removing it from the jig.

I created the two abutments from sheet styrene. I made them in an angle that matched the bridge's diagonal shape. Before continuing, I checked that the bridge had enough clearance for any type of train. I determined the height of the abutments by adding the height of my tallest piece of rolling stock, a double stack container car,

with the height of the roadbed and track. Finally, I attached the abutments and the center support to the bridge.

Painting and weathering

The next step was painting the bridge. With my airbrush, I gave it several coats of concrete color starting with the underside. I mixed my own concrete color from equal amounts of Model Master Flat Gull Gray, Sand, and Flat White. An alternative concrete color is Vallejo 71045 US Light Gray. This paint comes close to producing a warm gray concrete color right out of the bottle.

After the paint had dried, I stained the bridge with several washes made from equal amounts of Woodland Scenics black and Stone Gray Liquid Pigments Earth Colors mixed with plenty of water and a few

drops of rubbing alcohol. The washes gave the very uniform gray surface a more dirty used look.

Next, I painted a double yellow center line on the roadway. I cut thin strips of masking tape to mask the outline of the stripes first and then filled the masked area with yellow paint.

In addition to the wash, I weathered the bridge with black and brown powdered chalk. On the abutments, beams, and guardrails, I applied the chalk with a soft brush. On the roadway, I used a sponge to smudge the powder down the center of each lane.

The chalk adheres very well to the flat Model Master paint, so I didn't give the bridge a sealing coat of varnish. If a structure will undergo a lot of handling, I would seal it with Vallejo Flat Finish or a similar varnish.

The photo shows the finished bridge installed on my layout. From this angle, the slightly arched shape is more noticeable.

TUNNEL PORTAL

Just before the track enters the east end of the staging below Daneville, it makes a big curve into a little canyon and disappears into a tunnel. I wanted a tunnel portal for my tunnel that matches the type seen in the Tehachapi Mountains, so I had to make it myself. The easiest way would have been to make it from styrene, but making one of plaster produces a more-realistic concrete look.

I began by making a mold out of styrene for the tunnel portal as well as one for the tunnel walls, or liner. If the tunnel is cut through hard rock, the inside walls will be pure rock, but if the tunnel is cut through more porous rock, the lining will be made of concrete.

For many years, I have used Woodland Scenics Lightweight Hydrocal for rock castings. This material is very easy to cut and carve, but it also breaks easily, and I was afraid it would be too soft for this purpose. Instead, I used alabaster plaster, which I found in an art supply store. This plaster dries harder than Hydrocal.

I poured the plaster in the styrene molds and poked a stick in the wet plaster along all edges to make sure that the plaster came out in all corners of the molds.

The plaster hardened within 10 minutes, and I removed the castings from the molds after 15 minutes. Even though the casting was still damp, it was surprisingly strong. The alabaster plaster set very smooth, almost with a surface like marble, so I gave the castings a light sanding to give them a rougher concrete look.

Painting and weathering

If you want your tunnel portal to have a newly constructed look, paint it a concrete gray color and then give it a couple of light black washes. If you want your portal to look older, you will get the best result by staining the white plaster with several washes. I made a wash from equal amounts of Woodland Scenics Slate Gray and Raw Umber Liquid Pigments and applied it to the castings.

The tunnel portal casting is shown here with two of the liner sections attached.

Before adding the stain, I dipped the castings in plain water. If you apply the stain to a dry casting, the casting will soak up the stain, and you will end up with plaster that looks too dark. It is much easier to control the intensity of the color on a damp casting. The color will dry lighter, so you can make the castings a little darker than you want the final result to be. I gave the parts three or four washes and set them aside to dry.

To complete the weathered look, I added some soot, in the form of black powdered chalk, above the tunnel entrance and on the tunnel walls.

Installing the tunnel

I positioned the tunnel portal on the layout and ran a test train, featuring double-stack cars and a 90-foot auto rack, through it to be sure that there were no clearance problems before I secured it with a few dabs of lightweight plaster.

I installed the liners on one side first. When the engineer on my test train had approved the position of the liners, they were fastened with lightweight plaster. I let everything set before I installed the liners on the other side.

Making your own molds and tunnel castings

1. I first made a mold for the tunnel portal from .040" styrene. I reinforced the entrance with styrene supports.

2. I then made a mold for the tunnel lining. I invented this system to hold the curved styrene sheet in place until the glue had dried.

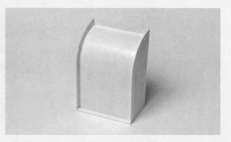

3. On this finished mold for a half tunnel section, the shape of the curve matched the tunnel entrance.

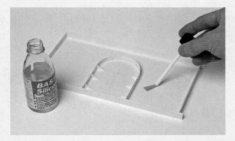

4. The next step was to cast the pieces. To prevent the casting from sticking to the mold, I first brushed it with a thin layer of silicone.

5. I filled the mold with alabaster plaster, a hard type of plaster, and inserted a stick in the wet plaster along the edges to make sure that the plaster spread to all corners of the mold.

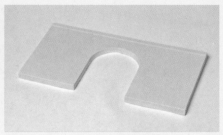

6. The plaster hardened within 10 minutes, and the casting was removed from the mold after 15 minutes. Even though it was damp, the casting was surprisingly strong.

7. I also brushed the liner mold with a layer of silicone prior to applying the plaster. Allow the silicone to dry before you fill the mold with plaster.

8. Because the liner mold is not flat but curved, I added less water to the plaster to get a thicker mix and quickly filled the mold using a spatula.

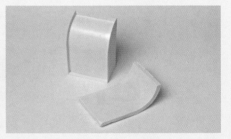

9. I made a total four wall sections for my tunnel. I didn't apply additional silicone to the mold between each casting. The initial coating worked for all four castings.

10. I gave the portal several washes made from water and equal amounts of Woodland Scenics Slate Gray and Raw Umber Liquid Pigments.

11. The liners received the same treatment. I sanded both the portal and the walls with fine grit sandpaper before I stained the parts.

12. I finished the weathering by adding some soot in the form of black powdered chalk above the tunnel entrance and on the tunnel walls.

ASPHALT TRANSFER TERMINAL

I was searching for a small, interesting-looking rail-served business for the new Daneville. From my old layout, I was going to move a warehouse that received boxcars and the plastic pellet transfer facility that received hoppers. In addition to running those cars, I enjoy operating tank cars, so an industry that was served by tank cars would be perfect.

I don't keep my old issues of *Model Railroader*. I give them away after I have read them, but first I cut out articles that I think could become useful some day, and that turned out to be a good idea. While browsing through those old articles, I came across a story about building a liquid asphalt transfer terminal from February 1994 by Clyde B. Maybee.

According to the article, the facility receives the liquid asphalt in insulated tank cars. At the unloading area, the asphalt is heated in the tank cars by steam and then pumped directly into waiting trucks. Since the tank cars are used as storage, space-consuming external storage tanks are not necessary.

Although handling liquid asphalt sounds like a messy business, it is handled

The truck loading platform weighs trucks as they are loaded.

A pickup truck is parked near the heat exchanger that heats the liquid asphalt with steam and the pump section.

A sandbox under each tank car catches spilled asphalt.

very cleanly, and the model should reflect that tidy look.

The facility was perfect for my needs: it had an interesting and complex look, the product it made was hauled by tank cars, and it would fit the available space on my layout. Liquid asphalt is mainly used for paving and roofing, so a facility such as this one would be at home on any modern layout.

I generally followed the guidelines in Maybee's article, except for a couple of minor improvisations along the way. I used various dimensions of Plastruct tubes for most of the piping.

In the article, Maybee explained how he bent his tubes over a candle flame. That method definitely did not work for me, so after I had used up a whole package of Plastruct tubes without having made a single useful bend, I gave up and ordered a bunch of Plastruct elbows instead.

For the support columns and the truck loading platform, I used various pieces of Evergreen strip styrene that I had on hand. I also made good use of my scrap box, where I found ladders and items that I used for valves and other parts. For the concrete block walls of the office buildings, I used Concrete Wall Sections from Pikestuff.

The two storage tanks are both from Walthers. The small one is from the Industrial Tank Detail Set and large one is from the Black Gold Asphalt kit.

Most details were applied before I painted. Only details that would be too difficult to paint at their location were painted first.

I glued most of the parts with styrene cement except when I glued Plastruct parts to Evergreen parts. For that, I used cyanoacrylate adhesive. Even though both are made from styrene, they didn't bond very well with cement. Gluing Plastruct parts together with cement worked fine, so I assume that Plastruct and Evergreen uses different types of styrene and, for some reason are not compatible.

Painting the model

I constructed the model as several sub-assemblies for easier painting (see photos on page 86).

All the general piping is made as one section, and I painted the pipes with Model Master Chrome Silver as suggested in the MR article. The chrome color was too shiny for my taste, so I also gave the pipes a coat

The local switcher in Daneville has picked up a string of empty tank cars at the liquid asphalt transfer terminal to move them to the yard in Daneville.

The facility is shown from above. The main building contains the office and two boilers. The big tank stores a chemical that is added to the asphalt, and the small tank contains boiler fuel.

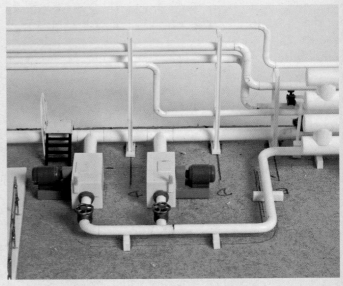

1. The truck loading platform is mainly made from various types of Evergreen strips. The staircases are from Plastruct.

2. The asphalt pumps are made of styrene sheet. The piping and the green motors are Plastruct parts.

To make the installation easier, the structure is built on a sheet of medium density fiberboard.

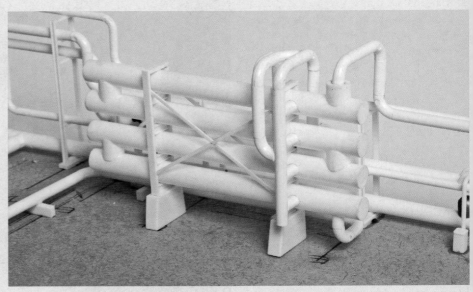

5. The black ladders are from my scrap box, and the handrail is made from .005" x .005" styrene strip.

6. The heat exchanger is made from Evergreen tubes. The connecting piping is from Plastruct tubes. I used three different dimensions of Plastruct tubes for the structure: ³⁄₃₂", ¹⁄₈", and ³⁄₁₆".

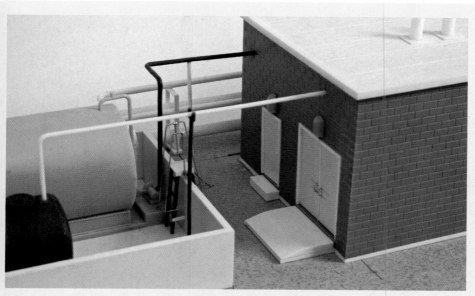

3. Details at the back of the office building include scratchbuilt doors and lamps above the doors, which are pieces of plastic sprue.

4. The valves are also scratchbuilt from parts I found in my scrap box.

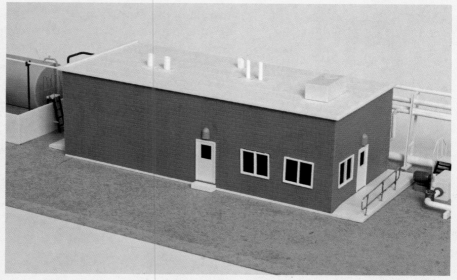

7. The black steps are more parts from my scrap box. The handrail is made from .005" x .005" styrene strip.

8. The office building is made from Pikestuff concrete block walls. The windows and doors are also from Pikestuff. The tar-paper roof is made from strips of self-adhesive paper.

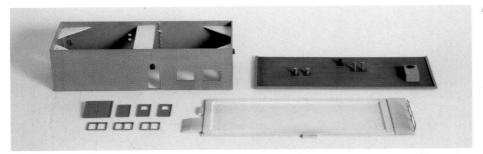

The main building consisted of subassemblies to make painting easier. I also didn't mount the windows before the painting was done. I painted the walls a brownish gray color mixed from Model Master tan and Gull Gray. Doors, window frames, and roof trim were painted with Model Master Italian Sand with a drop of Leather for a more brownish tone.

I made these lamps for the facility from a set of Faller street lamps and some Rix telephone poles. The arm for the light fixture is Evergreen styrene rod that I bent over a candle flame. I painted the pole as I did my telephone poles (see page 71).

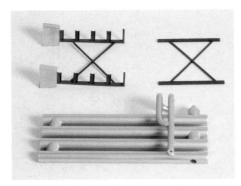

The heat exchanger and its support columns were also painted separately before the parts were assembled.

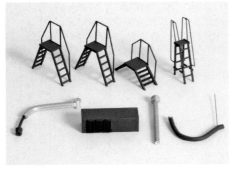

Ladders and other small parts were painted before they were installed.

of Vallejo Flat Finish to kill some of the shine.

In Maybee's article, the office building was shown with blue walls. I wanted to give my building a more typical Southern California color, so I painted it a brownish-gray color. The color was a mix of Model Master tan and Gull Gray. Doors, window frames, and roof trim received a coat of Model Master Italian Sand with a drop of Leather to give it a more brownish tone.

The truck loading platform was built on a sheet of styrene. I made the roof removable, so I could paint it separately. I first sprayed the platform gray. Then, I masked everything except the sides of the ladders and sprayed them yellow. I brush-painted the handrails yellow as well. The two storage tanks and truck scale were painted with Model Master Engine Gray.

Installing the model

The structure was built on a piece of medium density fiberboard (MDF) that fit the available space on my layout. After all the painting was done, I installed glazing in the main building's windows. I assembled everything and attached the main building, truck loading platform, heat exchanger, and other pieces to the MDF base. The complete structure was then attached to the layout with screws.

I applied, wet, and glued the ground cover to the area. I started with the dirt and then added the ballast. The facility not only uses ballast for the railroad track but also uses it under the piping and at the pump area to keep the areas clean. At one end

To simulate the sheets of tar paper on each side of the sandbox, I used pieces of paper towel soaked with thinned Model Master Engine Black. I used 3M Display Mount to glue them to the ballast. I attached the paper towel pieces to the sticky part of a Post-It sheet before I sprayed them with glue.

The truck loading platform is built on a sheet of styrene. I made the roof removable, so I could paint it and the platform separately.

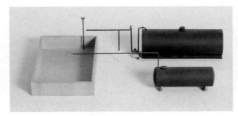

The storage tanks were not glued to their base until everything had been painted.

The tar paper is in place as are the hoses. The hoses are made from different sizes of solder that is easily shaped to look like soft rubber hoses.

Completing the area

1. The entire structure was built on a sheet of medium density fiberboard, so it was easier to install on the layout. After the installation was complete, I applied ground cover and ballast.

2. I used a shaker to apply the ground cover. A shaker is not a very precise tool, so a lot of dust and sand ended up on the piping. I used a soft brush to wipe it off.

3. When the entire area had been covered with dirt and ballast, I dripped water mixed with rubbing alcohol on it until everything was wet.

4. I then went over the area one more time with thinned white glue and let it dry.

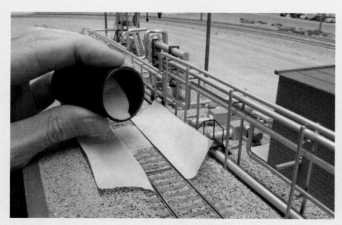

5. Each tank car in the unloading area has a sandbox underneath it. I attached a piece of stripwood at each end of the sandbox and filled the area with fine Cajon Sandstone from Arizona Rock & Mineral. To avoid getting sand in places where I didn't want it, I applied masking tape to the top of the rails.

6. I then wet the sand with a water-alcohol cocktail followed by diluted white glue.

Building a sturdy chain link fence

1. From the Walthers fence kit, I used the fence posts and drilled holes in them for the brass wire. This is best done while they still are on the sprue. To make sure that the brass wire and the pole will create a 90 degree angle, you have to be careful to hold the drill completely vertical.

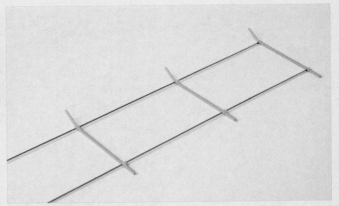

2. After removing the posts from the sprue, I slid two .019" brass wires through the top and bottom holes and secured them with cyanoacrylate adhesive (CA). On the long sections, I used several pieces of brass wire. I made the joint by sliding the first wire halfway through the hole in the post and then pushed the next wire into the hole from the other side and secured the joint with CA. It is best if the upper and lower wires don't join in the same post.

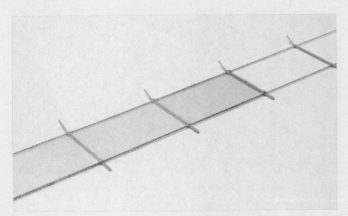

3. With a pair of scissors, I cut the brass mesh into appropriate strips and glued the mesh to the wires and posts with CA. Let the pieces overlap a little at the joints. To make them as invisible as possible, I made joints at posts.

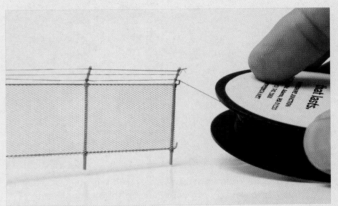

4. To simulate the barbed wire usually found on top of chain link fences, I attached three strings of EZ-Line, an elastic string made by Berkshire Junction. I twisted the lines around each post and applied a dab of CA to the joints.

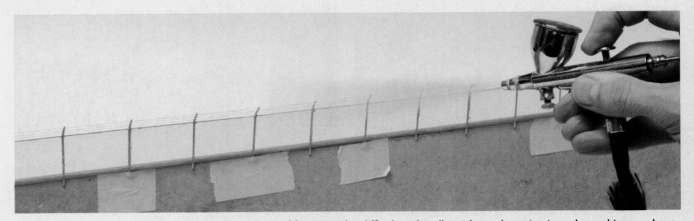

5. I painted the fence a light gray color. A long piece of fence can be difficult to handle without damaging it, so I taped it to a sheet of medium density fiberboard before painting it.

I used Walthers Chain Link Fence kit as a starting point but combined it with Detail Associates .019" brass wire and Scale Scenics brass mesh to obtain a sturdier fence.

of the facility, a storage bin contains fresh ballast.

When the entire area had been completely covered with dirt and ballast, I covered the area with water and a little rubbing alcohol and again with thinned white glue.

Each tank car in the unloading area has a sandbox underneath it. I attached a piece of stripwood at the ends of each sandbox

and filled the masked areas with fine Cajon Sandstone from Arizona Rock & Mineral.

I let it dry for a few days before applying the last details, which included sheets of tar paper on each side of the sandboxes and hoses at every unloading area.

I made the tar paper from pieces of paper towel painted with Model Master Engine Black. To create the hoses, I shaped pieces of solder to look like soft rubber hose and painted them black.

A fence for the facility

The asphalt transfer facility is protected by a chain link fence. I made the fence by combining parts from various manufacturers. The posts came from a Walthers Chain Link Fence kit. The mesh was from Scale Scenics, and the brass wire came from Details Associates. Scratchbuilding the fence produced a sturdier fence than those I could find in manufactured kits.

I drilled a series of holes in the layout for the fenceposts. I then took a section of fence and applied a small drop of white glue to the bottom of each post and placed the section

It is crucial that the mounting holes for the fence are drilled very precisely. I made a drilling template from a piece of cardboard. I placed the fence on the cardboard and marked every hole with a pencil. I then placed the template on the layout and drilled the holes. After the first hole was drilled, I stuck a pin in it to prevent the template from shifting while drilling the rest of the holes.

in the holes. I worked with one section at a time, starting with the long section running along the full length of the facility. I then moved on to the gates and other sections.

Finally, I added a few weeds and shrubs here and there, and the facility was ready to receive its first tank cars.

Making gates for the fence

1. The facility contains a pair of gates at both ends for truck traffic, and one end has an additional pair of gates for a track.

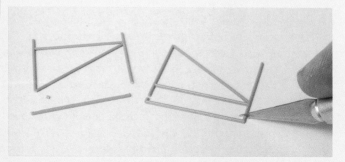

2. To clear the track, one set of the gates had to be trimmed. To do so, I cut out a small piece of each vertical bar of the gates and glued the bottom bar back on.

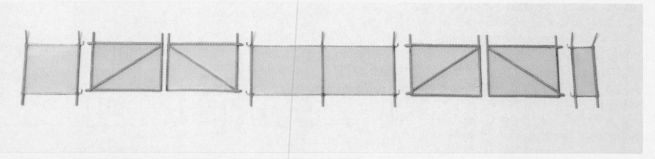

3. The gate section at the left includes the track gate with the higher clearance, while the gate at the right is for the truck entrance and has not been modified.

BEST DEAL AUTO

The redesigned Daneville layout provides room for an extra structure at the east end of town next to the Best Value Inn. In Daneville's sister town, Mojave, Calif., you will find a Ford dealership on that particular spot. A car dealership could definitely make an interesting scene, but since I model the present time, having a car dealership could easily become a costly affair. I would have to renew the inventory from time to time to keep it updated, and model cars are not cheap.

Instead, I killed two birds in one stroke. I simply turned the Ford dealership into a used car dealership. Not only didn't I have to worry about supplying new cars for the dealership all the time, I now had a place to put all the vehicles I had replaced over the years with newer cars to keep my layout current.

Parts for many of the structures in Daneville had been cut on a milling machine from drawings I made on my computer, but as I didn't have easy access to the milling machine anymore, I decided to make the dealership the old-

fashioned way—with handcut styrene sheets and strips. To my surprise, it took me only two evenings and a Sunday afternoon to finish the project, including painting, which was much quicker than I had managed to build any of the other buildings in Daneville. Creating a drawing for a milled building would take me several days, and additional time would be needed for the milling itself and then for the assembly.

I loosely based my structure on the Ford dealership in Mojave. I first searched my scrap box for parts that I could use and found a set of windows and a door—the rest had to be made from scratch.

I didn't make precise drawings of the structure to work from. All I drew was a rough pencil sketch.

Armed with a sharp hobby knife, I cut out the base and then the walls, ceiling, and roof. I glued the walls to the base and then built up

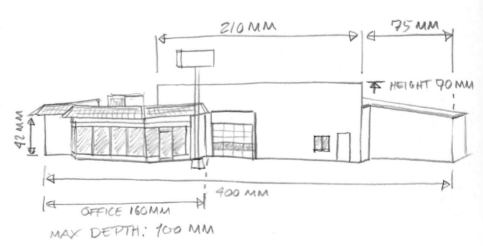

Scratchbuilding the dealership

1. Best Deal Auto is similar to the other buildings along Daneville's main street as it is not a full building. It is what I call a back-drop building because it is just a few inches deep and placed against the backdrop. The structure was made the old-fashioned way: scratchbuilt with handcut parts made from styrene. I assembled all the parts and glued them with liquid cement applied with a brush.

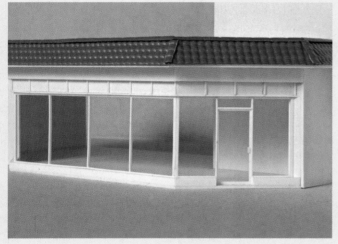

2. The office was the most complicated part of the structure to make. The window frames and trim were made from assorted styrene strips (see cross section on the next page). The roof was made from a Plastruct plastic sheet of Spanish Tile.

3. The tar paper on the shop roof was made from self-adhesive paper cut in strips applied to a styrene sheet.

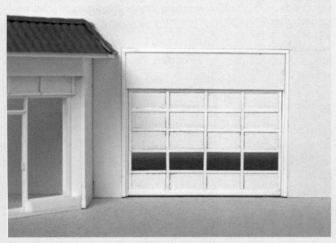

4. The garage door was made from a thin sheet of styrene with styrene strips glued to it.

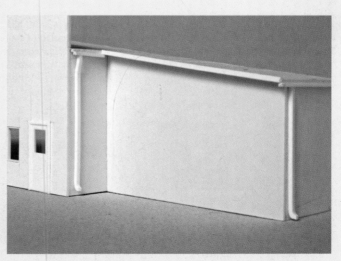

5. The downspouts are leftovers from a Pikestuff kit, and the gutters are made from Evergreen channel styrene strips.

Office cross section

Plastruct Spanish Tile

.020" x .250" styrene strip

Roof
.040" styrene sheet

.020" x .250" styrene strip
.040" styrene sheet
.020" styrene sheet
.020" x .020" styrene strip

.125" x .188" styrene strip

.040" x .040" styrene strip

Ceiling
.060" styrene sheet

.200"

.885"

Window frame
.020" x .040" styrene strip

.100" x .100" styrene strip

Base
.040" styrene sheet

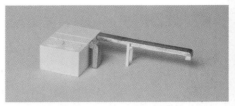

The air conditioner and ductwork were from Great West models.

the window section in the office from various styrene strips, as shown in the cross section.

I made the garage door from a thin sheet of styrene and styrene strips. The garage door frame was made from styrene strips. I didn't glue the garage door, window, and small door to the shop yet to make painting easier.

The roof tiles on the office were made from a Plastruct Spanish Tile plastic sheet. The tar paper on the shop roof was made from self-adhesive paper cut in strips.

The air conditioner and ductwork on the roof were from Great West Models.

Painting the structure

The first step was to re-create the stucco seen on many buildings in California. For that, you need some very fine sand and a clear acrylic varnish. I painted the walls with varnish and sprinkled fine sand on the wet varnish. The roof on the office received the same treatment. When the varnish had dried, I wiped the walls with a dry brush to remove any loose sand.

I sprayed the walls with a light beige color mixed from Model Master Sand and white. Almost all colors used for this building are custom mixed to match the

prototype. The reddish-brown color used on the garage door, shop door, and trim was mixed from brown, red, and white. I used Model Master Gull Gray for the window section in the office.

I had a Humbrol 70 that came very close to the color of the roof tiles. Adding few drops of white and red made it perfect. The tar-paper roof received a coat of warm dark gray mixed from dark gray and brown. The roof on the office was painted in Humbrol 140.

The air conditioner I airbrushed with Model Master Gull Gray, and I weathered the grilles with some black chalk powder to give them some depth. I also gave the air conditioner a dab of rust here and there.

Finishing steps

After everything had been painted, I installed the window glazing. Most windows in California buildings are tinted, and I applied a tinting film, bought in an auto parts store, to a clear styrene sheet before I cut the pieces for the glazing. The garage door, air conditioner, and small parts were glued in place.

I made signs for my auto dealership on my computer and printed them out on self-adhesive paper. I applied them to thin styrene sheets and glued them to the sign post and then on the building.

I installed the structure on my layout and filled the parking lot in front of it with tempting offerings for the residents of Daneville.

Creating stucco

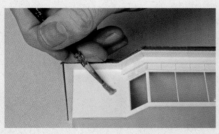

1. To re-create the stucco seen on many buildings in California, I first applied a layer of clear acrylic varnish to a wall section.

2. I then sprinkled fine sand on the wet varnish. I repeated the process on the remaining wall sections until everything was covered with varnish and sand, including the roof on the office.

3. I wiped the walls with a dry brush to remove any loose sand, and the building was ready for painting. I didn't glue the garage door, window, and small door to the shop at this point. It is easier to paint these parts before they are attached.

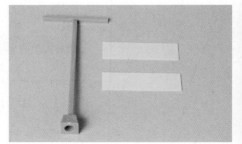

The sign post was made from a H beam that I found in my scrap box and pieces of styrene.

Painting the building

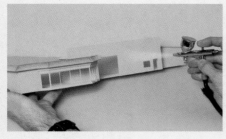

1. I airbrushed the walls in a custom-mixed light beige color. I used Model Master Sand and white enamel paint, but you can use any type of paint as long as it is flat.

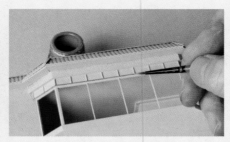

2. I brush-painted the trim around the windows in a reddish-brown color mixed from brown, red, and white.

3. I used Model Master Gull Gray on the window and door frames in the office.

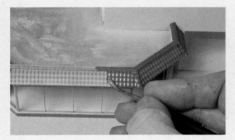

4. The roof tiles received a coat of Humbrol 70 with a few drops of white and red added to lighten it a bit.

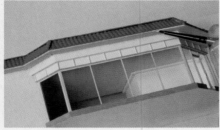

5. I painted the trim under the roof and gutters an aqua green color.

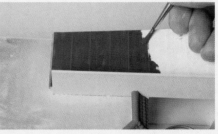

6. The tar-paper roof received a coat of warm dark gray mixed from dark gray and brown.

7. I painted the roof on the office with Humbrol 140 Gray. After the paint had dried, I applied brown and black powdered chalk to give it a weathered look.

8. The garage door and shop door was airbrushed with the same color I used for the trim around the windows in the office.

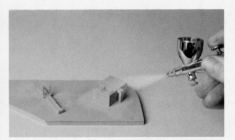

9. I airbrushed the air conditioner and ductwork with Model Master Gull Gray.

10. I worked some black weathering powder into the grilles to make them stand out. I also gave the air conditioner a dab of rust here and there.

11. I made the signs for my auto dealership on my computer and printed them out on self-adhesive paper. They were applied to thin styrene sheets and glued on the building and to the post. To finish, I applied the window glazing. I coated a sheet of clear styrene with a tinted film before I cut the pieces for the glazing.

LASER KIT HOMES

The residents of Daneville live in laser-cut wood kit homes. There are plenty of these types of kits on the market to choose from, and they generally all follow the same concept. The kits are pretty straightforward to build and look nice too. Laser-Art Structures offers a nice selection of typical American homes that will fit in several different eras. One of the kits I selected from that company was the Callahan House.

I recommend painting most of the kit's parts before assembling the model except for walls, which I painted after gluing together. The window frames, doors, and trim are peel-and-stick parts. The easiest way to paint a whole bunch of windows and doors is to cut the parts from the trim sheet and attach them to a sticky surface. I simply glued a large label to a piece of cardboard with the sticky side facing up. I then placed the window frames, doors, and other small parts on

the label's adhesive side and gave them several coats of paint with my airbrush.

Assembling the model was easy due to the large number of self-adhesive parts. For assembling parts that are not peel and stick, I used ordinary carpenter's white glue.

I didn't use the roof shingles that came with the kit. They looked fine but needed to be glued to the roof. Instead, I used self-

adhesive roof shingles from Laser Kit since the self-adhesive shingles were easier to apply.

The only problem in using wood structures on a layout is that water will ruin them, so you can't place them on the layout until the surrounding scenery has been added. After the scenery was completely dry, I placed the buildings on styrene foundations that I had made and glued to the layout earlier.

I glued down styrene foundations for the houses before adding scenery. I installed the wood houses after the scenery was completed to avoid any damage to the structures from the water used while adding the scenery.

Building and painting the kit

1. I first assembled the walls using white carpenter's glue. White carpenter's glue dries slowly so make sure the corners are exactly 90 degrees as the structure is left to dry.

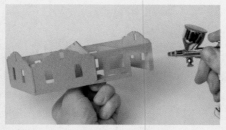

2. I painted the walls a light beige color. It required several coats to cover as the wood absorbed the paint. For wood kits, I prefer enamel colors since acrylics have a tendency to make the walls warp.

3. When the paint dried, I sanded the painted surface carefully to remove the coarseness of the wood, and then I applied a final coat of paint to the structure.

4. I painted the windows, doors, and trim separately in another color. To make that job easier, I glued a large label, sticky side up, to a piece of cardboard and removed the backing paper.

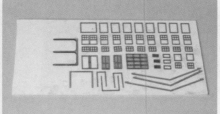

5. I placed all the parts to be painted white on the sticky label. Of course, this method only works for parts that don't need to be painted on both sides.

6. I sprayed everything white. Since all the parts were wood, I used a solvent-based paint, which required several coats to cover the parts.

7. I applied the window glazing and assembled the windows. I also applied the brick foundation to the structure. I first painted the foundation a warm gray color and then stained it a darker gray to add depth.

8. I didn't use the shingles that came with the kit as they required gluing. It was simpler to use peel-and-stick shingles from Laser Kit. Painting the shingles required a two-step process. First, I painted them light gray with Humbrol enamel paint.

9. After the gray dried, I brushed on a stain made from Vallejo Cam Black Brown mixed with some water and rubbing alcohol.

10. I applied the last trim parts, and I also added some extra details from my scrap box such as this utility meter.

11. An air conditioner is a must when you live in Daneville, and fortunately, I had one in my scrap box that I could use.

12. The house is now finished and ready to be installed on my layout. All in all, it only involved a few hours work and some drying time to build and paint the kit.

YARD OFFICE

The Union Pacific employees in Daneville needed a place to work in, and the modern yard office made by BLMA seemed to be a good choice. The model comes assembled and has a distinct plastic look to it that was easily changed by a light weathering. I also added a few extra details to the office.

It would have been easier to weather the structure if I removed the window glazing first, but it was glued tight, and I was afraid that I might break either the glazing or the window frames if I tried to separate them with force. Instead, I covered the window glazing with masking tape.

To cut pieces of masking tape to the correct sizes, I measured all the windows and drew their contours on strips of masking tape. I masked all windows and gave the building a light spray with Model Master Sand thinned to a wash consisting of one part paint to two or three parts thinner). After this dusting, I sprayed on a coat of flat varnish (Vallejo Model Matte Varnish) to kill the plastic shine. I then applied some brown and black powdered chalk with a soft brush to all the surfaces, careful to not apply too much powder to the white walls. Chalk is much more visible on a light surface than on darker ones.

There is no interior in the building, so you can see right through it. Since the yard office is located in the foreground of my layout, and highly visible, I made some interior walls to block the view. The walls were easy to make from pieces of styrene sheet, and I used strip styrene for the door frames. I didn't bother painting the walls but painted the doors a warm brown color.

It can be hot in Daneville, so an air conditioner was essential for employee comfort. In my scrap box, I found a white metal air conditioner from Great West Models. I mounted it to the wall with styrene strips.

I also added an electrical cabinet made from a small styrene block. I crafted a door for the cabinet from a .005" styrene sheet and added a handle from my parts box. To simulate the electrical cable going into the cabinet, I glued a round styrene bar to the bottom of the cabinet

I then airbrushed the air conditioner and electrical cabinet with Model Master Gull Gray. I worked some black weathering powder in the grilles of the air conditioner to make them stand out.

I glued these details to the yard office building along with a radio antenna tower made by BLMA.

For the final detail, the office needed a sign announcing that the office belonged to the Union Pacific, so I made a small UPRR sign on my computer and printed it out. I glued the paper sign to a piece of .010" styrene, cut it out, and glued it to the wall.

Detailing the yard office

1. I masked all window glazing with small pieces of masking tape and gave the building a light spray with Model Master Sand thinned to a wash. To kill the plastic shine, I gave the entire building a coat of Vallejo Model Matte Varnish.

2. I weathered all the surfaces with some brown and black powdered chalk. I was careful not to apply too much with a soft brush since chalk is more visible on lighter surfaces.

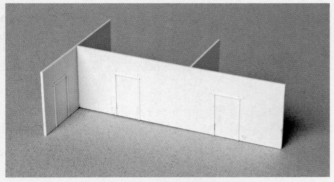

3. Without an interior in the building, you can look right through it. I made interior walls from pieces of styrene sheet to block the view and added door frames made of strip styrene to the walls.

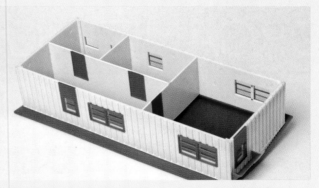

4. It wasn't necessary to paint the white styrene walls, but I did paint the doors and door frames brown before I glued the walls in place.

5. I used a white metal air conditioner from Great West Models to cool off the office and glued it to wall mounts made from styrene strips. I made the electrical cabinet from a small styrene block and added a cabinet door made from .005" styrene with a Overland Models door handle. I attached a round styrene bar to the cabinet for the wires. I made the UPRR sign on my computer, printed it out, and glued it to .010" styrene.

6. I airbrushed the air conditioner and electrical cabinet with Model Master Gull Gray and then rubbed some black weathering powder in the air conditioner's grilles to give them some depth. After gluing the parts to the building, the yard office was ready to serve the UP employees in Daneville.

ORGANIZING WIRING

If you had looked under my old Daneville & Donner River layout, a spaghetti bowl of wires would have met your eyes. Not even the color coding was consistent. I had ambitiously started out with specific colors of wire for the different purposes, but when I ran out of a color, I just used what I had instead of driving to a hobby store and buying the right color. That didn't make my old layout very service friendly, so I swore that on my next layout I would make my wiring impeccable.

Organize your wiring

In the local building supply store, I found some plastic channels in different sizes meant for hiding electric wires. They consist of a U-shaped channel and a cover that snaps on. With a peel-and-stick mount, they would be easy to attach to benchwork. They seemed perfect for organizing my wiring, so I bought a bunch of them. I mounted the channels on the edge of the hidden staging and below the main line. All the wiring runs through the channels until it reaches its point of destination.

I took no shortcuts in the color coding this time—every type of item has its own color of wiring. It took me a few trips to the hobby store to buy new supplies, but

it was worth it. Now, I don't have to be ashamed of anything if visitors take a look under my layout, which they, for some reason, always do.

Control panels

Another wiring element that needs to be done on a new layout is turnout control. The control panels are very exposed on the fascia, so I wanted the control panels to look nice and match my silver-colored aluminum Lenz connector panels.

I had to make three control panels: one for the tracks in Daneville, one for Duolith Cement, and one for the hidden staging. I prefer using metal for my control panels as it is more rigid than styrene, so I used 5/64" thick (2mm) sheets of aluminium.

With my computer, I made schematic drawings of the track arrangements and printed them out on my laser printer. I glued the prints to the aluminium sheets using 3M repositionable spray mount. Using the prints as templates, I drilled holes for all the toggle switches. On the panel for the hidden staging, I wanted lights to indicate which way the turnouts are set, so in addition to the holes for the toggle switches, I also drilled holes for two 3mm LEDs per switch. There was no need for indicator

lights on the panels for Daneville and Duolith Cement as all the turnouts there are visible.

After all the holes were drilled, I removed the prints and cleaned off glue residue from the aluminium surfaces with thinner. I painted the panels flat black using a spray can. I re-created the track arrangements with masking tape and sprayed the panels silver.

I removed the masking tape and gave the panels a protective coat of satin varnish.

I use Tortoise switch motors for my turnouts, and they need DC power and operate by switched polarity, so I mounted toggle switches on my control panels. I soldered all the wiring to the toggle switches before mounting the panels to the fascia on my layout.

I mounted plastic channels on the edge of the hidden staging. All wiring runs through these channels. The cover is easily removed if you need to access the wires.

Making aluminum control panels

1. I made each control panel from a ⁵⁄₆₄" sheet of aluminium cut to the correct size.

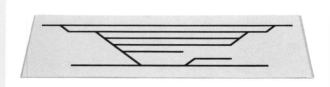

2. I made a schematic drawing of the track arrangements, in this case for Daneville, on my computer. I printed out the drawings and glued them to the aluminium sheets using 3M repositionable spray mount.

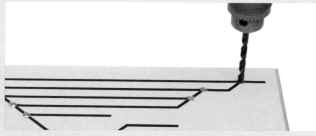

3. Using the print as a template, I drilled all the holes for the toggle switches.

4. After all holes were drilled, I removed the print and cleaned glue from the surface of the aluminium with thinner.

5. I spray-painted the panel flat black and let it dry.

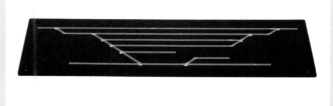

6. I re-created the track arrangement with masking tape using the holes for the toggle switches as guides.

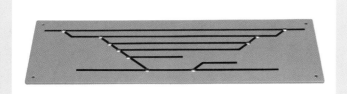

7. I then spray-painted the panel. After removing the masking tape, I coated the panel with satin varnish.

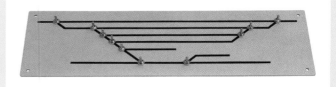

8. I installed the toggle switches in the predrilled holes on the panel. I soldered all wires to the toggle switches before I attached the panel to the fascia.

I hope you have found both inspiration and useful information on the pages of this book.

It has been just as much fun building Daneville the second time around as it was building it the first time. While building the layout, I used proven techniques, worked with new types of scenery materials, and did some things in totally different ways. My backdrop is a good example of that. It is always exciting to see how something you have never done before turns out, and I learned a lot from creating my first photographic backdrop.

My overall ambition was to make a better version of my beloved Daneville, and in that, I have succeeded. When I compare photos of my old Daneville layout with the pictures I took of my new layout, there is no doubt in my mind that the new layout is superior to the old one in all aspects. I am especially pleased with my stretch of desert that probably is as close as I can get to re-creating the feeling of the vastness of a desert on a 20"-deep scene.

Most model railroaders I have talked with couldn't understand why I wanted to tear my first Daneville layout down to build it again, but rebuilding it has been a kind of therapeutic process for me. I proved to myself that I could do better, and that has given me peace of mind. It might sound odd to many of you, but I am ready to let Daneville go now—the Daneville chapter can be closed as far as I am concerned. Not that I want to tear my layout down right away, but my interests lie in creating layouts or dioramas. When a project is finished, I become less interested in it, and my mind begins to scan for new challenges. When I start on a new project, and what the theme will be I don't know yet; all I know is that it will happen eventually.

Pelle K. Søeborg

List of materials

TRACK

Peco (www.peco-uk.com)
SL8381   Code 83 #8 Turnout, right hand
SL8382   Code 83 #8 Turnout, left hand

Micro Engineering (www.microengineering.com)
10104   Code 83 Flextrack, wood ties
10105   Code 83 Flextrack, concrete ties
10106   Code 70 Flextrack
10108   Code 855 Flextrack
14705   Code 83 #6 Turnout, left hand
14706   Code 83 #6 Turnout, right hand
14805   Code 70 #6 Turnout, left hand
14806   Code 70 #6 Turnout, right hand
30104   Spikes, medium
30106   Spikes, small
26055   Rail Joiners, Code 55
26070   Rail Joiners, Code 70
26083   Rail Joiners, Code 83

SCENERY

Arizona Rock & Mineral (www.rrscenery.com)
130-2   Ballast, NP Medium Gray
138-2   Ballast, CSX/SP
11003   Low Desert Soil

ASOA (www.asoa.de)
1710   Gneisschotter

Silhouette (www.mininatur.de)
727-23   Long Tufts, Early Fall
727-24   Long Tufts, Late Fall
737-23   Two Color Grass Tufts, Early Fall
737-24   Two Color Grass Tufts, Late Fall
990-23   Horse Tail, Early Fall
990-24   Horse Tail, Late Fall

Woodland Scenics (www.woodlandscenics.com)
ST1452   Smooth-It
ST1455   Paving Tape
C1201   Lightweight Hydrocal
C1230   Rock Mold Outcroppings
FL632   Static Flock Grass, Harvest Gold
C1218   Earth Colors Liquid Pigments, Stone Gray
C1220   Earth Colors Liquid Pigments, Black
C1222   Earth Colors Liquid Pigments, Burnt Umber
C1223   Earth Colors Liquid Pigments, Yellow Ocher

DETAILS

Berkshire junction (www.berkshirejunction.com)
1471HB   EZ Line
1471OB   EZ Line

BLMA (www.blmamodels.com)
4105   Concrete Grade Crossing
4101   Radio Antenna Tower

Details West (www.detailswest.com)
GT-916   Ground Throw Switch
SM-903   Switch Motor and Tie Mount

N.J. International (www.njinternational.com)
525-1172   Crossing Gates

Pikestuff (www.rixproducts.com)
541-0013   Highway Guardrails

Rix Products (www.rixproducts.com)
628-0030   Telephone Poles
628-0035   Clear Crossarms for Telephone Poles

Sunrise Enterprises
111002   Single Target Signal
111052   Dual Target Signal

Scale Scenics (www.circuitron.com)
652-3501   Micro-Mesh, brass

Walthers (www.walthers.com)
933-3304   Cantilever Crossing Signal
933-3125   Chain Link Fence

STRUCTURES

BLMA (www.blmamodels.com)
4300   Yard Office

Great West Models (www.greatwestmodels.com)
110   One-Story Office

Laser-Art Structures (www.branchline-trains.com)
604   Callahan House
622   Whitehall House

Laser Kit (www.laserkit.com)
126   Mrs. Williams House

NuComp Miniatures
871005   Mobile Home

Rix Products (www.rixproducts.com)
628-111   Modern Highway Overpass

Scale Segmental Bridge
T-girder Type 2 Segmental Bridge

Walthers (www.walthers.com)
933-3081   Plastic Pellet Transfer

About the author

Pelle relaxing at Hill 582 in Cajon Pass.
Photo by Ken Perry

Pelle K. Søeborg, a Danish resident, runs his own graphic design business. In the early '90s, several *Model Railroader* magazines caught his attention, and he has been a model railroader ever since. A trip to the United States in 1992 added to his interest in modeling United States prototypes.

In 2006, *Mountain to Desert*, his book about his home layout, was published. It was followed by *Done in a Day* and *Essential Model Railroad Scenery Techniques,* all published by Kalmbach Books.

Pelle has also written a number of articles for *Model Railroader* magazine throughout the years and has provided photos for model train calendars and for Woodland Scenics and Walthers catalogues.

Index

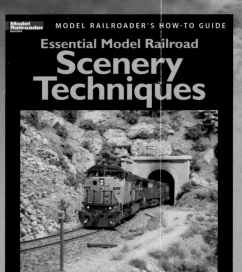
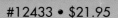
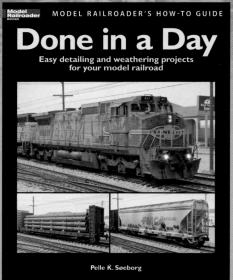